OUR
CONSTITUTION
MADE EASY

RICHARD BRITNER

WESTBOW
PRESS®
A DIVISION OF THOMAS NELSON
& ZONDERVAN

WestBow Press books may be ordered through booksellers or by contacting:

WestBow Press
A Division of Thomas Nelson & Zondervan
1663 Liberty Drive
Bloomington, IN 47403
www.westbowpress.com
844-714-3454

ISBN: 978-1-6642-0831-5 (sc)
ISBN: 978-1-6642-0832-2 (hc)
ISBN: 978-1-6642-0830-8 (e)

Library of Congress Control Number: 2020919639

Print information available on the last page.

WestBow Press rev. date: 10/22/2020

CONTENTS

★ ★ ★

CHAPTER ONE

THE START

Most books start off with an introduction, but if most people are like me, they want to cut to the chase and just start in at chapter 1, so I thought I should just incorporate the introduction in chapter 1 as this book isn't your typical book.

First, this was never supposed to be a book. When I started this project, I was attempting to write scripts for a series of YouTube videos. It seems to me that most people today would rather watch a video than read a book. The latter method is just too time consuming and lacks stimulation. I believe the information in this book is of the utmost, dire need for patriotic Americans to have, so I wanted to get it out in the way I believed was the most effective method possible.

Of course that method was YouTube.

I am not a techie, but even I appreciate the value of learning via others' experience and seeing the proof of their knowledge firsthand. I coupled the scripts with a series of articles I wrote for the Tea Party and planned to attach them to my YouTube page so they could explain in greater detail what I covered in the videos.

My hope was that the videos would spark a greater interest in our Constitution so viewers would be willing to take the plunge into

1

the world of the written page. What talent I have lies in the written medium, so writing the scripts and articles came easily for me.

Then came what turned out to be the monumental task of producing the videos. Through that experience, I realized that I was by no means an actor or producer. It took me only eight months (and a friend who reviewed one of what I thought was a complete video) for me to come to that conclusion. After those eight months of work, all I really had was scores of bloopers that would have landed me first prize on *America's Funniest Videos*.

I still, however, believe that the information I want to convey is vital for the well-being of this nation and our people. It is imperative if we wish to remain a free people or more accurately regain our freedom. As harsh as that sounds, we are slaves to our government. So I decided to fall back on the medium I was confident with and decided to write this book.

At first, I got the idea of leaving those as scripts and individual articles and put them in chapters, but after a proofread, I realized it was too chaotic. I realized I would have to reorganize my scripts and articles and write new chapters in the traditional method incorporating it all into new and more-complete articles.

You're going to notice some redundancy. Actually, I'm very happy with that because with repetition, inculcating as it might be, there's a greater chance that you'll remember what I wrote. I hope what I wrote will drive you to be a more active participant in securing our liberty.

I felt the need to write a book, or articles and scripts, about the US Constitution because I understand the subject; I fully understand what our founding fathers were trying to establish for us—a nation in which everyone could live independent and free, devoid of excessive governmental control. A nation in which there was little government, only what was necessary to keep us safe from invasion and maintain a civilized environment. A nation whose government officials were our servants, not our masters. This is why we call our legislators, our members of the judiciary, and executives civil servants, not leaders.

We were never meant to have a president who was the leader of this nation; he was meant to be only the leader of the federal government. Our Congress was never meant to be the leader of the federal government; its members' only job is to make laws. The only, 'quote,' oversight authority given them is the oversight of their own house.

Yes, the Senate can approve or deny a treaty. Yes, it can approve or deny the selection of a presidential selectee or appointee. But that is the extent of its constitutional authority as it pertains to oversight. Anything beyond that is an act of rebellion.

Nor are our federal judges to be leaders over us; it is illegal for them to make case law as I will reveal later in this book. Their only job is to decide the case before them, and their ruling is exclusive to that case.

As Tomas Jefferson stated in his letter to the Danbury Baptist Church, "The legitimate powers of government reach actions only, & not opinions." Yet the government we have today, and I'm talking about government at all levels, as our master, freely makes laws that are designed to curtail what we think in direct violation of the supreme Law of the Land. Let me give you a clear example of how our so-called leaders in the federal government are clearly exceeding their true authority and enslaving the people.

The Affordable Care Act, better known as Obamacare, is a federal law that forced people to obtain health insurance. This law was illegal on so many levels that it becomes ludicrous. One, the president has no authority to demand that Congress make any type of law. Second, health care is a public act, and Congress has absolutely no authority whatsoever to make a health care plan for the people let alone make it law. Third, the Supreme Court classified health care as a tax knowing very well what it was ordaining was extortion. All of this I will clarify later in this book. But think about this, how does health insurance make health care affordable? The only way to make health care affordable is to make it affordable. The Democrats pushed this bill not for the sake of the populace but to enrich the insurance company tycoons. This is the only thing this bill did, and let me add that the Republicans were behind this act all the way.

So what did I mean when I stated that the only way to make health care affordable is to make it affordable? When the Democrats first started clamoring about health care, I knew that it was illegal for them to do so but that they would accomplish their task. Knowing that, I wrote my House representative Rep. Dennis Rehberg and laid out a plan that would actually make health care affordable. Here's my letter.

To the Honorable Dennis Rehberg
Dear Congressman Rehberg,

I would like to discuss the topic of socialized medicine. Please forgive me if I sound a little condescending in this letter; it is not directed at you personally. We both know that the fourth article of the Constitution gives the State government full authority over public acts and that medicine is a public act. But we both know quite well that the federal government has not abided by the Constitution for decades. We also know quite well that if the Democrats institute social medicine, and they will, that they will do more harm for the nation than good.

What I propose instead of Socialized Medicine is that we institute Monopolized Medicine. Please hear me out. I know how some people feel about monopolies. The federal government would have full authority over the monopoly with the States being the overseers. If the federal government had over twenty employees in the system, then there would be too much federal involvement as well as too much administrative involvement. As you are aware of, the purpose of socializing medicine is to reduce the cost and make it affordable for the people. Administration is a no-profit portion of business. There is a small need for admin, but it is not cost effective.

What I propose is that the federal government controls every aspect of the medical field. From education, practice, research and development, pharmaceutical, to emergency response.

Medical school would be controlled by the government. They would own the buildings, supply the doctors to be the teachers, and supply the curriculum. The school would only focus on medicine, and other electives would not be given. Students should have received a well-rounded education in high school and not need any more rounding in med school. They should strictly focus on learning to heal. This will reduce the cost of schooling, which in turn will reduce the stress of paying back student loans. Meaning we do not have to pay them as much before they can get their feet on the ground.

Doctors as well as all other medical staff would be paid on a GS schedule. An intern would be paid a GS-10 salary. A one-year resident would jump up to a GS-12, and a three-year resident would jump to a GS-13.

A doctor who excels and becomes a surgical specialist would be given a GS-14, and a doctor who is nominated to become a teacher would be given a GS-15 grade. This will promote competition and provide cost-effective treatment for the people. As you know, these pay grades provide for a comfortable living, not rich, but comfortable.

Nurses, med techs, and pharmacists would attend the same schools, different courses with less time and money, and also be paid on a GS schedule. The salary range would be from GS-7 to GS-10.

Paramedics, first responders (EMTs), and aides would be trained at the hospitals and be paid at the GS-6 to GS-8 range.

Psychologists, not psychiatrists, would be paid at a GS-10 to GS-11 schedule. As psychologists primarily just listen to people's problems and most people need to get a lot off their chests, there is more time spent at these offices, and most just render bad advice in the first place. Therefore, the lower salary will make it affordable for the people especially if they are truly neurotic.

No doctor or nurse would be put in an administrative position. Persons trained for administration work will do that type of work. A file clerk or receptionist would be a GS-5 to GS-6, and the hospital director would be a GS-12.

As with socialized medicine, health insurance will need to be abolished in monopolized medicine as well. I will not go into details, but health insurance was a bonehead idea in the first place, and is the root cause for our souring health cost.

The reason monopolized health care will work in reducing the cost is because the government controls the price tag and the pricing would look something like this.

A doctor visit: The average time spent in a doctor's office, not including your waiting time, is about 20 minutes. You pay a minimum of one hour at $32.00 per hour for a GS-12 doctor. You pay a $10.00 administration fee that covers the handling of paper work, swabs, and the paper that lines the examination table. Total cost for visit, $42.00.

Lab work: The cost of a doctor's visit, $42.00, the lab technician, GS-8 at $18.00 per hour for two hours, the lab material actually used at $40.00, and an admin fee of $10.00. The total cost for a doctor visit and lab fees is $128.00.

Surgical procedure: A two-hour procedure with a specialist surgeon at GS-14 is about $42.00 per hour. Two nurses and anesthesiologist GS-8 at $18.00 per hour. The cost for the anesthesia, oxygen, and other surgical supplies $50.00. Admin fees $10.00, plus a profit margin of 10% and the total cost of the surgery is $277.20.

Overnight hospital stay of 12 hours: A flat fee for the room would be $75.00 per night. This is the average cost of a hotel room. Then there are the nurse's fees, but these are a reduced rate as the fee is dispersed among the other patients she/he attends, let's say $5.00 per hour. Cost of medicine; this is the exact cost of each pill, not the bottle, $15.00 and $10.00 for a one-time admin fee. The total for the night is $160.00.

Emergency room treatment: The cost for the doctor for two hours of treatment is $64.00. The nurses and attendants, figure three of them, $108.00. Medical supplies $50.00, figuring paying for just what is used. Admin cost, $10.00. Total cost for a trip to the emergency room, $232.00.

Trip in ambulance: Cost for two EMTs at GS-7, $15.00 per hour, one hour minimum $30.00. $.50 per mile, from home to hospital, let's say 6 miles, $3.00. Medical supplies, oxygen, IV (mostly water and salt) and bandages, $50.00, vehicle maintenance $15.00. Cost of vehicle $50.00. Total cost of trip, $148.00.

How to determine the cost of a medical procedure or device, such as a c-scan, X-ray, or ultrasound.

Let's say you need a c-scan (sorry, I don't know the technical term) and the machine costs $1,000,000.00. The life span of the machine is five years and in five years it will be used on 250,000 patients. 1,000,000.00 divided by 250,000 is $4.00 per use. Double that and the exam should cost $8.00. The reason you double it is so you pay for the unit and after the five years have enough to buy the next machine outright. The next five years, after the initial first five years, $4.00 of the test goes to replacement costs and the other $4.00 is profit. After five years a nice profit is made.

Assisted living: A flat fee of $800.00 per month for apartment, this price at 2008 cost of living. On staff, nurse GS-9 at $19.50 per hour, plus other attendants such as cooks, activity organizers, etc. at GS-5 or 6. All of these personnel's salary fees would be dispersed among all the residents. Then add a profit margin of 5%.

Nursing homes should be figured the same as the assisted living but a CNA GS-7 for every six patients. The monthly rent should only be about $400.00

As you can see, no combination of these procedures costs over a $1,000.00 making a monopoly a very cost effective form of medical health care. Since the primary concern of the government is the health and welfare of the people and not making a large profit for shareholders, the people should never be gouged.

The pharmaceutical companies would be controlled by the monopoly as well. From the research and development, manufacturing and distribution, all should be controlled by the government. The cost of medication should be figured by the cost of development and manufacturing and a cost recoup of 10 years. After ten years a medicine's cost can be lowered, but now kept at a small profit margin.

Some of the profits should go to maintenance of the facilities, but much will go into a benevolence fund. Those people who do not even make minimum wage can apply for this benevolence. In this fashion, this monopoly actually takes on the form of a socialized system, but in fact, most people will be paying on an as-used process and not be taxed to death. We'll get enough of that when we pay off this mindless bailout. Oh, by the way, the bailout won't work. The reason recessions or depressions come is to equalize the economy. With that bailout, the equalization never happens. Thus, it just prolongs the agony.

I'm sure you realize that you could never call this a Monopolized Health Care plan; the Democrats would be shocked and dismayed. Probably many Republicans as well. Democrats are less into substance and more into phonetics. 'If it sounds good, it's marvelous, darling.' So if you choose to consider this proposal, my suggestion is you call it a Post Modern Socialized Medical Health Plan. It has a lot of big sounding words and very politically correct. They should buy off on it.

Please give this proposal some serious consideration. I think if you truly think about what I'm proposing, you will see it is for the benefit of the American people. It is far better than the socialized medicine that the Democrats want to impose on us. Thank you for your time and consideration.

Sincerely,
Richard Britner
Clancy, MT

You see, to make health care affordable, you have to reduce the cost, not force people to buy insurance. Our government cares nothing about the people; it is interested only in pleasing those who put money in their pocket. By the way, Rehberg wrote me back and stated that they already had a plan they wanted to pass. At that time, the Republicans were still claiming to be fighting the bill. Come on, people. It's time we the people stop being so gullible and educate themselves. Hence, I put my scripts and articles in this book. I incorporated my scripts into these new articles, but I left my introduction script for the YouTube video in its entirety as seen below. Hope you like it. Happy learning.

Oh ya, I need to give special thanks to Abe and Johnette Gonzales, and Ralph Coia for their help with this project. Thanks guys

YouTube Scripts

INTRODUCTION

Hello. My name is Richard Britner, and what I'd like to do for you is present a series of tutorials on our US Constitution that I've entitled "Our Constitution Made Easy." There are many myths today concerning our Constitution, and I want to give you a clear picture of what our founding fathers were truly trying to do for us when they penned our Constitution.

It was not to empower our federal or state governments, far from it. Their purpose was to ensure that we the people would always remain free. They did so by setting in place restrictions and limitations. The only way for a people to remain free is by placing limitations on their government, a set of boundaries it cannot cross. So you make a law binding the government and making it a criminal act if it breaches those limitations. We call that law the Constitution.

So how did I obtain my expertise on this subject? In 1991, the US Treasury Department sent me to the federal police academy to become a US Mint police officer. As you would think, the academy had an extensive course on constitutional law.

At that time, they explained the four branches of government outlined in the Constitution and their functions, how the legislative was the most powerful branch of the federal government, the executive was the second most powerful, and the weakest branch of the federal government was the judiciary. They also explained how state governments were sovereignties in themselves and had a symbiotic but essential relationship with the federal government.

In 1996, when I transferred to the Federal Protective Service, I was sent to the same academy again. That time, however, the training on the Constitution was not as extensive and they were teaching that there were three equal branches of government and that the Constitution placed certain restrictions only on the state government—the antithesis of what I had previously learned.

Federal police officers are sworn to uphold the Constitution, and as I was taught two differing explanations of the same document, I, being an autodidact, decided to conduct an investigation to determine what version I should be enforcing. These videos are the result of what I learned from that investigation.

What I'm about to teach you will be totally different from what your college law professor taught you or what you learned in high school. So how can I be sure what I'm teaching you is the truth about our Constitution while all the constitutional scholars are getting it wrong?

Our founding fathers left nothing to chance. And three of the men who wrote the Constitution also wrote a series of articles known as the Federalist Papers. These articles explained in explicit detail why they wrote the Constitution, the way they did it, the purpose of the Constitution, the functions of the various branches of government, and why they placed the limitations on it that they did. They left no room for misinterpretation of the Constitution. Any deliberate misinterpretation of the Constitution by any branch or agency of the federal government or for that matter any level of government is a criminal act. It is a crime, an act of rebellion, for them not to follow the letter of this law.

Throughout these tutorials, I will define certain words in the Constitution. The only way anyone can truly understand the Constitution's meaning as our founding fathers understood it and intended for us to understand it is to know the definitions of the words they used as they knew them. The only reliable dictionary we can use then has to be one written in the same era they wrote the Constitution, the *American Dictionary of the English Language* by Noah Webster, 1828. In it are the definitions of the words exactly as the founding fathers knew them and intended them to be used.

I'd like to share with you a creed I learned as a child written by Dean Alfange. I believed in it then, and I believe it more so today.

> I do not choose to be a common man. It is my right to be uncommon. I Seek Opportunity to develop whatever talents God gave me – not security. I do not wish to be a kept citizen, humbled and dulled by having the state look after me, I want to take the calculated risk; to dream and to build, to fail and to succeed. I refuse to barter incentive for a dole. I prefer the challenges of life to the guaranteed existence; the thrill of fulfillment to the stale calm

of utopia. I will not trade freedom for beneficence nor my dignity for a handout. I will never cower before any earthly master nor bend to any threat. It is my heritage to stand erect, proud and unafraid; to think and act myself, enjoy the benefit of my creations and to face the world boldly and say – "This, with God's help, I have done." All this is what it means to be an American.

I hope you find my tutorials educational, and if you like them, please subscribe to my site. If you are interested in knowing how we came to our present political state, I have written a novel, *Dark Side of America*, that explains how we went from a free people to a nation with masters. You'll find it on Amazon or at Barnes & Noble or Redemption Press at the link below.

I have also written a series of articles explaining our Constitution in greater detail, so please read these attached articles. Until next time, may the blessings of the Lord be on you.

CHAPTER TWO

ARTICLES 1–3

Article 1: What Our Founding Fathers Didn't Want

> I know of no safe depositor of the ultimate powers
> of society but the people themselves: and if we
> think them not enlightened enough to exercise their
> control with a wholesome discretion, the remedy
> is not to take it from them, but to inform their
> discretion by education. This is the true corrective of
> abuses of constitutional power. —Thomas Jefferson

My name is Richard Britner, and I'm a former inspector with the Federal Protective Service, part of the Department of Homeland Security. I wrote a series of articles explaining our Constitution in hopes of helping people gain a better understanding of what our founding fathers were trying to set in place for the American people. Some of the things I say are most likely going to be contrary to what you have been taught and contrary to some of your core beliefs, but please don't be offended. I ask you to be objective as you read these articles and to cogitate on what I'm saying. After looking at all the evidence I present and applying logic and reason, determine for yourself if what I am teaching makes sense.

In these articles, I use the words *uneducated* and *uneducation* but not with their traditional meanings. In addition to my being a former federal law enforcement officer, I am also a writer with two books published at this time. In my second book, *Plight of Cody Stein,* I neologized a definition of the word *uneducated*: the intentional teaching of false or erroneous information or partial teachings; neglecting to teach all pertinent information with the intent of indoctrinating a false worldview. This is not a reflection on a person's intellect. When I use the term *uneducated,* I am not referring to a person who is ignorant or unschooled; I am referring to a person who has been schooled incorrectly.

Before we can take a serious look at what our founding fathers were trying to set in place for the American people, we need to look at what our founders did not want for us. If you ask most people today what system of government we have here in America, they will tell you a democracy. And why wouldn't they? That's what is being taught in our high schools, colleges, and universities, and the press and media profess us to be a democracy every chance they get. Even at the capitol in Washington, DC, our elected officials shout democracy.

Democracy was developed in ancient Greece and the word *democracy* is derived from the Greek words *demos*—people—and *kratein*—to possess or govern. So the literal meaning is people's government or people's rule. What makes a government a democracy is self-representation. If you represent yourself in the making of proposals for laws, voting on those proposals, and enforcing those laws, and everyone else represents themselves similarly, you have a democracy.

The definition I'm about to read is from the *American Dictionary of the English Language* by Noah Webster, 1828. This is very important to understand because as you can tell by the year it was written, the definitions are identical to the founding fathers' understanding as they drafted the Constitution. This is the only reliable dictionary we have today when trying to understand the Constitution and the intent of our founding fathers. Modern dictionaries are plagued with revisionism and are therefore unreliable sources. A prime example of what I am talking about is the word *democracy*. Here is the definition from the Noah Webster dictionary of 1828.

> Government by the people: a form of government, in which the supreme power is lodged in the hands of the people collectively, or in which the people exercise the powers of legislation. Such was the government of Athens.

Notice there is no mention of representatives or the people voting for representatives. Yet in revisionist dictionaries, they add, "a society where the people freely vote for their representatives in a democratic election." That's hogwash! Whenever you have representatives, you have a republic. Our founding fathers were educated men who knew the distinctions between forms of government. Today's politicians and scholars are desperately trying to obscure those distinctions, and it is not for the good of the people. But this article is not about sociological manipulation, so I'll get back on track. Whenever I give a definition of a word, it will be derived from the Noah Webster dictionary of 1828 so you will have a true understanding of what the founding fathers had in mind.

In a true democracy, a law is proposed and the community votes on it, and with a majority vote—51 percent to 49 percent—the bill passes or fails. Majority rule is not exclusive to democracy; all forms of government apply the majority rule when passing laws. Let's say we have a plutocracy and the ten richest men in the world are actually running this government. On day one, the members introduce a bill to this committee of ten to abolish Christianity, and it comes to a vote. Four vote in favor of the bill but six vote against it because they don't believe now is the time to abolish Christianity. So the bill fails due to the majority rule, six to four. Majority rule is just common sense and not indicative of democracy.

The most important question to ask is, What did our founding fathers think of democracy? Let us take a look at the writings of a few of our founders to determine if democracy was the form of government they would have wanted for us.

The first of our founding fathers we will take a look at is James Madison, a representative from Virginia, one of the developers and signers of the Constitution and one of the three authors of the Federalist Papers. Everything I'm about to teach in these articles can be verified through the Federalist Papers. This is what Madison had to say about democracy.

> Democracies have ever been spectacles of turbulence and contention, have ever been found incompatible with personal security or the rights of property and have in general been as short in their lives as they have been violent in their deaths.

Not a very high opinion of democracy, is it? Next, let us look at what Alexander Hamilton had to say. Hamilton, a representative out of New York, was a developer and signer of the Constitution and another author of the Federalist Papers. This is his opinion of democracy.

> We are a republican government. Real liberty is never found in a despotism or in the extremes of democracy.

Hamilton was putting democracy on the same level as despotism. Ouch!

Let us take a look at another founding father's view of democracy. Samuel Adams was one of the developers and signers of this nation's first constitution, the Articles of Confederation. He had this to say about democracy.

> Democracy never lasts long. It soon wastes, exhausts and murders itself.

Harsh words. Our founding fathers disdained democracy because they were actually highly educated men. They had studied the history of the Greek city-states. For democracy to work, you must have complete conformity; there can be no tolerance for diversity. Although conformity is required in all forms of civilized society, it is paramount in a democracy. Sooner or later, a bill was passed into law that was a benefit to the larger percentage of the people but was harmful to the rest. And instead of conformity, they chose conflict, and these conflicts were usually settled with the edge of a sword. This is why our founders used terms such as "murders itself" and "violent in their deaths."

It becomes obvious that our founding fathers had no intention of establishing a democracy for this nation. We never were, and I hope we will never be. Yet we are led to believe in our high schools, colleges, universities, in media and even at our nation's capital that we are a democracy. Why? Would you ever challenge a government you were supposedly in charge of?

When democracies crumble, they fall into a state of anarchy. Some scholars list anarchy as a form of government derived from the Greek *anarchia*—meaning to rule. People do what they want with impunity. There is no supreme power. There are some who believe that this is a good thing. They are under the illusion that somehow people are all just going to get along. Nowhere in history can you find societies that just got along. Where you have a gathering of people, you will always have those who want to take advantage of the weaker. This is why where anarchy reigns, you soon get the establishment of a structured government. This is why in history, so many have used anarchy as a tool to establish themselves as the ruling body. When society crumbles, the people are offered a new order, and this new order will come in the form of an autocracy or oligarchy. I want to look at autocracies first.

Actually, monarchies get a bad rap in this country. Monarchies are actually the most efficient and effective form of government. In all other forms of government, you have to deal with committees in which egotism rather than intellect prevails. In committees, there is compromise where no compromise is justified, or petty squabbling and in most cases unnecessary litigation. The worst part of committee government is the division it creates. In a monarchy, a good monarchy, the ruler takes counsel, looks at the viable options, decides the best course action, and implements it. Simple. Effective.

In 1609, King James I of England gave a speech to Parliament on the divine rights of kings. It started out this way: "The state of monarchy is the supremest thing upon earth." He compared the attributes of a king to those of God and stated that a king is accountable to none but God. This is where the concept of eminent domain is derived from. He said,

> But just kings will ever be willing to declare what they will do, if they will not incur the curse of God … Therefore all kings that are not tyrants, or perjured, will be glad to bound themselves within the limits of their laws, and they that persuade them the contrary, are vipers, and pest, both against them and the Commonwealth.

The Bible confirms what King James said in the book of Daniel, in the description of King Nebuchadnezzar in 1 Samuel, David's treatment of Saul, and in Romans 13:4 (NIV), "He does not bear the sword for nothing."

If monarchies are such an effective form of government, why didn't our founding fathers establish one? Well, because of monarchs. Notice how King James stated that all kings who were not tyrants would be glad to bind themselves to the limits of their laws. Very few people in history who rose to the position of monarch have been good kings. And even if you start off with a good king, the next in line would most likely be a tyrant. This is how we came to the term *despot*. Few have ever wanted to rule over subjects in wisdom but preferred a slave/master relationship. Our founding fathers had had enough of that type of government.

Let's take a look at the other form of government, oligarchy, which means rule by the few. Committees. There are various forms of oligarchies: plutocracy, ruled by the rich; an example of this would be the one-world government. We have theocracy, ruled by religious rulers. (Note: religion is a belief or cause pursued with fervor and devotion. The god does not have to be the God of heaven; it can be a man-made god or idol.) Examples of this are some the Muslim or Islamic nations in the Middle East. But the oligarchies I would like to focus on are republics.

The word *republic* is derived from the Latin *res*, thing, and *populus*, public, meaning the thing of the people. There are various forms of republics such as Marxist republics (socialism, fascism, and communism). Examples most familiar to us are the old communist USSR (United Soviet [or Slavic] Socialist Republic), and the People's Republic of China.

What is the basis of Marxism? What is the underlying philosophy? You got it. I want it (business, wealth, prestige). I don't want to work for it. I don't want to take all the risks associated with starting a business. I don't want to put in the long hours with no assurance of extra pay. I don't want to take on the responsibility of employees. But you did, and now you have it, and I want it. Scholars say capitalism is based on greed, but Marxism in all its forms is based squarely on coveting. Covetousness is the evilest form of greed.

The claim of all Marxist, more commonly called socialist, leaders is that they are trying to make a society that is fair for all. Do you notice that our federal government has made special protected classes for groups of people? If there are certain groups of people placed in special protected classes, does that not imply that these groups are somehow inferior to those not needing special protection, that there are some people who are innately superior and other people who are innately inferior? Why else would there be such classes at all? The Declaration of Independence, the document that defines the character of this nation, states that all men are created equal. Ladies, don't get your feathers ruffled here. The word *men* is used in the same content as in Genesis 1:27 (NIV), where God said,

> So God created man in His own image, in the image of God He created him; male and female, He created them.

Both *men* and *man* are used to signify all humankind. There is no chauvinism here but your own. So if we are truly equal, why special protected classes? I will be readdressing this at the end of these articles; it might make more sense then.

Socialism is the form of government that takes control of private industry (not the economy; all forms of government affect the economy) through litigation.

Now it's my belief that Franklin Delano Roosevelt was the greatest traitor this nation has even known. FDR ran under the old Democrat Party platform but promised a new deal. That new deal was Marxism. FDR had a panel of advisors he called his think tank. These advisors were college professors who all professed to be Marxist. These are the men who guided FDR in turning this nation from being a free-market, constitutional republic into a Marxist republic.

When determining what form of government you actually have, you don't listen to what your politicians claim they are. You determine it by what form of politics they are practicing. Actions speak louder than words.

There are various levels of control, and each level has its own name. A socialist nation, being the lowest level of control, allows some ownership and control by the people who own and operate their own businesses. Still, there are laws in place to control them, and the executive officer mostly just enforces those laws.

The next highest form of socialism is fascism. The dictionary states that fascism is where a dictator and businesses become coleaders. This definition never made sense to me as it did not truly represent history, and communist leaders such as Lenin, Stalin, Mao Tse Tung, Castro, and Kim Jong-un were far more powerful dictators than Hitler and Mussolini were. Hitler had to use his courts to litigate laws he wanted passed because the German legislature was not cooperative enough.

The best definition I ever heard of fascism came from the John Birch Society: fascism is where the government controls the vast majority of private industry but gives the illusion of control to the people. This means the people operated the shops, paid the overhead, fixed the problems, and dished out most of the costs, but the government told them how to run their businesses such as by setting limits on the price of every item, making laws on whom and how to hire or fire, and everything else about their businesses.

The fascist nation most familiar to Americans was the National Socialist German Workers' Party, better known as the Nazi party. Oh, by the way, the National Socialist German Workers' Party was a union run amuck, and notice they were self-proclaimed Socialists. Hitler himself proclaimed to be a Marxist.

If you take an honest look at the policies of the Nazi party (see Halbrook, "Registration: The Nazi Paradigm" in the resource section), you'll notice today they parallel America's policies exactly. Hitler and the Nazi party were pro-abortion, claimed animal rights, promoted euthanasia, and were pro-homosexual (the vast majority of Hitler's SS officers were homosexual). They were pro-gun control, they persecuted Jews, Christians, and anyone else who disagreed with them, and used the media to propagandize. Hitler would legislate through litigation, and their economic policies were Marxist. Everything our government promotes today.

So why would Americas liberals want to change the definition of fascism? If your goal is to enslave the people, you don't want them to realize that your policies are identical to those of the most notorious government most Americans know. You redefine fascism, and then you claim that your opposition is fascist. After that, you redefine democracy because most Americans know democracy only to mean the people's rule, and you convince them through your propagandist to believe that what you are doing is for them and not to them. Now you know why the liberals have redefined democracy and fascism.

There was a YouTube site called Molon Labe Industries that did or does an excellent job of explaining the definition of fascism. You should look for it.

Have you noticed how liberal Democrats keep calling themselves progressive? Have you ever stopped to wonder what they are progressing to? A good Marxist always wants to progress to the ultimate Marxist state, communism. The highest form of Marxism is communism. Unlike fascism, communism makes no illusions about itself. The government owns everything, and the people are merely slaves of the state. The prime minister is defiantly a despot. Don't get me wrong; all forms of Marxism are slave/master relationships in which the people are the slaves and the government is the master, but with socialism and even fascism to a degree, the people retain some semblance of personal freedom. With communism, the slavery is complete. The executive is a despot (like Lenin, Stalin, Mao Tse Tung, Castro, and Kim Jong-un), and the people suffer. Slavery is obvious in communism.

The foundational principles of all forms of Marxism are based on the teachings of Karl Marx. A common trait of Marxism is thought control. In every form of Marxism, the rulers indoctrinate and demand that their people, their slaves, think their way. The stronger the form of Marxism, the more rigid the thought control. This is why you hear about political dissidents being imprisoned in communist countries.

So I have covered all the systems of government that our founding fathers were not trying to establish for this nation, systems of government they were trying to avoid like the plague. Not one of them guarantees freedom for the people, and some do just the opposite by their very nature.

The next article will address what our founders were trying to leave as a heritage for the people of this nation. What they desired was to make us a free people, but it was up to us to keep our freedom. —February 12, 2015

Article 2: A Look at a Constitutional Republic: What Our Founders Were Looking For

In my first article, *What Our Founding Fathers Didn't Want,* I gave a rundown on the various systems of government our founding fathers did not want the American people under bondage to; they did not want us to be a democracy, nor did they want us to be enslaved by any form of tyranny.

What they did want for us, as Alexander Hamilton stated, was a Republican government, and not just any form of a republic but a constitutional republic.

The definition of a republican form of government as understood and intended by our founding fathers is this.

> A commonwealth ; a state in which the exercise of the sovereign power is lodged in representatives elected by the people. In modern usage, if differs from a democracy or democratic state, in which the people exercise the powers of sovereignty in person. Yet the democracies of Greece are often called republics. —*American Dictionary of The English Language*, Noah Webster, 1828

This definition says it all—simple and complete.

What is a constitution? Robert Natelson, a former professor of constitutional law at the University of Montana in Missoula, gave a presentation in 2009 on the Constitution in Helena, Montana, at a Tea Party town hall meeting I attended. Natelson described a constitution as a set of rules designed to channel behavior for a specific outcome based on the rules. Our founding fathers understood this principle; they established the Constitution as a set of rules designed to channel the behavior of the government. Natelson said that the government could run properly only if those rules were obeyed.

This is an oversimplified explanation as to what a constitution is designed to do. Our Constitution is more than a set of rules or laws designed to channel behavior. The primary purpose of the Constitution is to act as a restraining device. When you think of the members of Congress, the president, and the Supreme Court justices, you should envision them all in shackles. The Constitution is designed to restrain them from going beyond the limitations set on them in it, which does not allow the federal government or any or its branches to arbitrarily ignore its confines.

So who is bound by the Constitution? Who is required by this law to obey it? Let's look at the Constitution itself for that answer. Article 6 states this.

> **Article VI.** - This Constitution, and the Laws of the United States which shall be made in Pursuance thereof; and all Treaties made, or which shall be made, under the Authority of the United States, shall be the **supreme Law of the Land**; and the **Judges in every State** shall be bound thereby, any Thing in the Constitution or Laws of any State to the Contrary notwithstanding.
>
> The Senators and Representatives before mentioned, and the Members of the several State Legislatures, and all executive and judicial Officers, both of the United States and of the several States, shall be bound by Oath or Affirmation, to support this Constitution; but no religious Test shall ever be

> required as a Qualification to any Office or public
> Trust under the United States.

The first thing I'd like to point out is that it states, "This Constitution, and the Laws of the United States which shall be made in Pursuance thereof …" This is a limiting clause. It allows Congress to pass only those laws that are pursuant to or in compliance with the Constitution, and only constitutional laws must be obeyed. It also states that treaties that are to be obeyed are to be under the authority of the United States. What is the authority of the United States? The Constitution. Again, this limits the president from making a treaty that does not conform to our Constitution.

But the laws and treaties that do conform to the Constitution and the Constitution itself are the supreme laws of the land. Supreme here means that it is the highest law in the land and all other laws are subject to it; no other laws can overrule the Constitution. And the land, as mentioned, is the entire United States; all state, county, and municipal government laws and ordinances must comply with the Constitution.

As proof, this article states, "The Judges in every State shall be bound thereby, any Thing in the Constitution or Laws of any State to the Contrary notwithstanding." This is a command that state, county, and municipal judges must conduct a judicial review of every law these legislators make to make sure they are in compliance with the Constitution. It is a crime if they don't do this.

Federal judges are not included in this clause even if their courthouses are in a state. I'll list you five reasons proving this. First, the clause was directed at the states. Next, it was never the intent of the founding fathers to have district judges. At first, they set up circuit judges that went from state to state to hear federal issues, but they quickly discovered that that was too arduous a task, so they set up district judges. Next, there is a matter of jurisdiction. Each federal courthouse is on exclusive jurisdiction like an island of federal property in a state but is not part of the state.

Next, it would violate the sovereignty clause in Article 4, Section 4 of the Constitution, and last, the power of judicial review over state law isn't given to the federal courts in Article 3. Every time a federal judge declares a state law unconstitutional, he is committing an unconstitutional and criminal act.

Article 6 requires the federal government (the president, Congress, and federal judges) to take an oath to support the Constitution, and it requires the same of the governors, legislatures, and the judges of every state. How could the founding fathers expect the state leaders to swear to support the Constitution if it didn't apply to them? This Article makes it clear that all governments are bound to this Constitution.

The founders wrote the Constitution in a way all citizens could understand. Back in 1788, the average person had an eighth-grade education; if you have an eighth-grade education, you have all it takes to understand the Constitution.

Daniel Webster, a congressman for both New Hampshire and Massachusetts in the early to mid-1800s, made this observation about the Constitution.

> It is hardly too strong to say that the Constitution was made to guard the people against the dangers of good intentions. There are men in all ages who mean to govern well. But they mean to govern. They promise to be good masters, but they mean to be masters.

The most important thing to remember is that our Constitution is a restraining device designed to keep our government under control. The second most important thing is that we can never remain free people if our government does not obey this Constitution. Supreme Court Justice Hugo Black had this to say about our Constitution in one of his more memorable quotes: "Our Constitution was not written in the sands to be washed away by each wave of new judges blown in by each successive political wind." He meant that the Constitution was not open for mere interpretation by judges.

In an interview with Walter Cronkite, Justice Black stated, "The Constitution is a literal document written by men who knew the literal meaning of words." The Constitution says what it means and means what it says. How else could it be?

Nowadays however, when you declare the Constitution to be a literal document, the vast majority of politicians, law professors, and federal agents roll their eyes, scoff, and call you a literalist with as much contempt and disdain as they can muster. As an average citizen, you're supposed to realize that taking the Constitution literally is ridiculous and foolish.

There's a name for those who claim the Constitution shouldn't be taken literally—traitors. It's nothing less than treason for a politician or any federal agent or teacher of the law to claim that the Constitution shouldn't be taken in the literal sense. For them to subvert the Constitution by misrepresentation is clandestine insurrection, treason. They are traitors to the Constitution, this nation, and to us, its people. Nothing good comes from their deception.

We are a constitutional republic held under democratic principles that the people are the true rulers of this nation and delegate their authority to the government. We the people. There are no shortcuts in saying this without losing sight of what our founders intended for us. I will expound on this later.

But our government is not operating on the good sense displayed by Justice Hugo Black; instead, it follows the philosophy of Chief Justice Charles Evans Hughes, who stated, "The Constitution is what the judges say it is," the antithesis of what Black preached.

I hope you recognize the dangers of this statement immediately.

As I mentioned in article 1, I went through the Federal Police Academy twice, once in 1991 for the Treasury Department and again in 1996 for the Federal Protective Service. I was given two theories of the Constitution, one in which the legislative branch was the strongest branch, the executive branch was not as strong., and the judicial branch was the weakest; they all had symbiotic relationships with state governments. In the other, I was taught that the three branches of government were equal and that the Constitution only put some limitations on state governments. How can you uphold a Constitution when you have been taught two entirely different versions of the same document? That prompted me to investigate what the founders of this nation expected of its civil servants. One of the first questions I needed answered was what other type of bad teaching I had received the second time around in the academy. Let's take a look.

> Lord Blackstone once commented that "the United States Constitution is the most remarkable document ever written by mankind, for the Constitution is constantly evolving to meet the requirements of an ever changing society. Judges, attorneys and law enforcement officials must realize that a study of the Constitution is never complete. It is subject to amendment by legislative action." ...

> This process is *obviously not the primary source of the Constitution's flexibility.* The manner in which it is viewed by the people at large, by the legislatures, and particularly by the United States Supreme Court, creates gradual, subtle changes in the way it is *interpreted.* ... It is not the Constitution that has changed, but the manner in which the courts have *interpreted* it. The Constitution is more than just the written document. In the words of the late Chief Justice Charles Evans Hughes, "The Constitution is what the judges say it is." —FLETC Law Text 1/96

I have italicized some of the text of my federal law enforcement training manual to draw your attention to certain phrases. Do you notice the assumptive speech in the second paragraph? I have a big problem with assumptive speech as do all criminal investigators; if you buy into the assumption, you accept the statement without any intellectual analysis.

Notice the name-dropping in the first paragraph—Lord William Blackstone, obviously someone of importance if they are dropping his name. Lord Blackstone was a renowned barrister, magistrate, and law professor in England in the mid to late 1700s. The vast majority of the lawyers in America in the 1700s had studied and learned and were influenced by his writings. If Blackstone made such a comment about the Constitution, you can pretty well take for granted that the statement is true especially when law is concerned. How much influence did he have in the development in this nation?

> ...to assume among the powers of the earth, the separate and equal station to which the Laws of Nature and of Nature's God entitle them ... — Declaration of Independence

This part of the Declaration of Independence is derived from his teachings. But is the idea of a law such as a constitution a constantly evolving concept that Blackstone would have endorsed? Let's look at some of his writings and see.

> As man depends absolutely upon his Maker for everything, it is necessary that he should, in all points, conform to his Maker's will. This will of his Maker is called the Law of Nature ... This Law of Nature is dictated by God Himself, is of course, superior in obligation to any other. It is binding over all the globe, in all countries, and at all times; no human laws are of any validity if contrary to this; and such of them as are valid derive all their force, and all their authority ... from this original. Upon

these two foundations, the Law of Nature and the
Law of Revelation, depend all human laws; that is to
say no human laws should be suffered to contradict
these. —Lord William Blackstone

Does this sound like the words of a man who supported an
evolutionary perspective of law? And was this just an innovative
belief of Blackstone alone? Before Blackstone, in the early 1600s,
Sir Edward Coke wrote,

The Law of nature is that which God at the time of
creation of the nature of man infused into his heart,
for his preservation and direction ... the moral law,
called also the Law of Nature.

This may sound like I'm digressing, but please bear with me.
Throughout history, all cultures have realized that laws have to be
taken literally, as they were written. An example from the Bible is in
the book of Daniel. King Darius was forced to attempt to execute
Daniel, who was a close friend and confidant despite the fact that he
did not want to. It was because of a law of the Medes.

Now, some christosphobes might be squirming right now with
all this talk of God and the Bible. But the fact is that over 30 percent
of the Constitution is derived from the Bible; it has been the template
for law for centuries. Just a few examples are the separation of powers,
found in Jeremiah 17:9; uniform immigration in Article 1, Section
8, derived from Leviticus 19:34; the number of witnesses for capital
punishment in Article 3, Section 3, derived from Deuteronomy 17:6,
and so on.

Some christosphobes claim that the Bible is an unreliable source
of information, that it is merely a bunch of made-up stories, that it
has lost its reliability through many decades of translations, or the
belief of Julius Welhausen and his higher critical thinking that the
Bible was written by more individuals at later periods of time than

the Bible claims making the writings less reliable. The problem for the christosphobes is that science, in particular archaeology, has put all these and any other arguments to rest.

If the Bible makes a claim about a certain event or references certain places and no archaeological evidence of that event or place can be found, you can make the assumption that the Bible is just a made-up story. For example, the Book of Mormon made claim to very large cities in North America such as Moronihah, Gilgal, Onihah, Mocum, Gisdiandi, and many others, but there is no archaeologist evidence of these large metropolises to support that claim. Also, the self-proclaimed prophet Joseph Smith claimed that when Nephi and his family arrived in America, they found horses, oxen, and donkeys, but we know that these animals were not indigenous to America; they were brought here by the Spanish in the 1500s. Because of the lack of empirical evidence and the fact that a known falsehood was claimed, we can safely surmise that the Book of Mormon is nothing more than a story told by a very talented writer.

However, as with the Bible, where there is a claim to a city that existed or an event that happened and when archaeological evidence is found that supports that claim, we are forced to concede that the Bible is true as written. You can't find empirical evidence of a made-up story, and the empirical evidence and external biblical writings can't support an improper or faulty translation of the Bible. The evidence just wouldn't match up. When 250 pieces of empirical archaeological evidence were found, the christosphobes should have been more careful about their claims about the inaccuracy of the Bible, but they weren't. When 2,500 pieces of empirical archaeological evidence and extrabiblical writings were found, the christosphobes should have realized that the burden of proof was on them to show that the Bible was unreliable, but they didn't. Now that there are over 25,000 pieces of empirical archaeological evidence and extrabiblical writings discovered supporting every aspect of the Bible from Genesis to the first three chapters of the book of Revelation, there is no legitimate argument against the fact that the Bible is one of the most reliable historical books. To make such claims to the contrary in light of all the insurmountable evidence is insane. We call this insanity christosphobia, the unreasonable and irrational fear of Christianity.

I know this sounds like I digressed, but all this information is pertinent to understanding the Constitution and our present political state and will become clearer at the end of these presentations.

Now back to the excerpt from the federal law enforcement training text. Blackstone clearly believed that laws were meant to be extensions of the permanent law of God; he was definitely not a fan of the concept of evolving laws. But in my training text he stated that the remarkable thing about the Constitution was its ability to evolve. That does not match up.

One other fact is necessary for me to point out to determine the reliability of this text and its intended teachings. The Constitution was written in 1787, ratified in 1788, and was not put into practice for all the world to see until 1789. Blackstone died in 1780. How did a man dead for nine years before he would have had a chance to see the Constitution in practice make such an eloquent commentary on the Constitution? Did the writers of the text hold a séance? This is an example of my definition of being uneducated. This revisionist view of history is designed to give the student a false worldview of our Constitution. But why? And where did this view that laws were every evolving come from?

In 1859, Charles Darwin came forth with his theory (hypothesis) of evolution in his book *On the Origin of Species by Means of Natural Selection, or the Preservation of Favoured Races in the Struggle for Life*, later shortened to *The Origin of Species*. In 1869, Charles Eliot became the president of Harvard University, and he was a fan of Darwin and his theory. In 1870, Eliot appointed Christopher Columbus Langdell as the dean of Harvard's law department despite objections from other law professors concerning Langdell's qualifications. The one qualification that mattered to Eliot was that Langdell was an evolutionist as he was. What a brilliant rationalization. Here is an excerpt of Langdell's case method concept.

> Law, considered as a science, consists of certain principles or doctrines ... Each of these doctrines has arrived at its present state by slow degrees; in other words, it is a growth, extending in many cases through centuries. This growth is to be traced in the main through a series of cases. —Christopher Columbus Langdell, 1870

Law is not science in the way Langdell defined it. Law is a process of learning acquired through experience, and then laws are designed for social stability based on what was learned. Laws are not as extemporaneous as Langdell implied.

What is meant by interpretation? Modern definition: when judges or lawyers have to interpret a law, it means that the law does not mean what they want it to say, but if they are to win their side of the argument, they're going to have to lie to you and see if you're gullible enough to swallow the manure they're feeding you. They are lying to you. If they say that the law says this or that, they have a case. If they have to interpret the law, it's guaranteed they don't have a case.

So if the federal law enforcement text is right and Langdell is right and laws are nothing more than the product of the evolution of court cases and public opinion, the intelligent person will ask, "Why do we need a legislature? We can save taxpayers a lot of money by getting rid of Congress." You think that our Senate and House of Representatives will go for that seeing how they would become obsolete?

Is there ever a time when a judge is justified in interpreting the law? Yes. It comes in the form of judicial review. In my next article, I will explain judicial review and how you and judges can determine if a law is constitutional or not.

What our founders established for us was a constitutional republic—a law, not a suggestion or a guideline but a law that was designed to restrain, limit, and rule over our federal and state governments to ensure our—we the people's—freedom.

—February 26, 2015

Article 3: Constitutional or Not

I started my first article with a look at the systems of government our founders did not want to establish. In my second article, I began to look at what they wanted, and I introduced you to a few ways the people were being purposely deceived so as to believe a false interpretation of the Constitution. I used a text from my federal police academy days to demonstrate my definition of uneducated, and I demonstrated a common misrepresentation of the court's authority in interpreting laws. I promised to explain how to determine if a law is constitutional.

What did our founding fathers want in our court system? King George's judges in the colonies were hearing cases brought under false charges and were conducting mock trials for the king's soldiers who committed all forms of crime including murder and were acquitting them. They were also striking down laws made by the colonists who tried to establish law and order in their communities. You can find this list of grievances in the Declaration of Independence.

In addition, King George would not allow the colonies to make laws regulating the courts. So when our founding fathers drafted Article 3 of the Constitution, they had a clear idea of what they wanted and more important what they did not want for our judicial branch of government.

Quite simply, courts and judges are to uphold the law. When a law is breached and charges are brought against a suspect, that suspect must stand before a judge and jury in a court of justice. It is the jury's job to review and weigh the evidence presented to determine the guilt or innocence of the suspect. It is the judge's duty to ensure that the trial is conducted in a manner as prescribed by law and maintain order in the court. When the jury renders a verdict, it is the judge's duty to acquit the suspect or sentence him to the proper punishment based on that verdict. That is pretty much it as far as the purpose of judges goes.

A judge has certain powers to conduct a trial as prescribed by law: to issue a warrant; to search, seize, and arrest; to issue a writ ordering an individual to comply with a legal court order such as a subpoena, summons, mandamus; to set bail; to render judgment; and to sentence a person convicted by a jury of his or her peers. Actually, this is a great deal of power when you think about it. But is it the job of the judge to interpret the law? Yes, but what does it mean to interpret? This means that a judge must determine what the legislature was trying to enforce and bind, not what he feels the law should say. When a judge interprets the law, he must determine the goal of the legislature. That is what matters, not his own opinion. But what if a judge feels a law is contrary to the Constitution? Can he disregard the law? Can he make that determination? This is called judicial review, the doctrine under which legislative and executive actions are subject to review and possible invalidation by the judiciary. Is there anywhere in the Constitution that gives the federal courts the power to conduct judicial review? Well nothing specific, but implied. Article 6, Paragraph 3 reads,

> The Senators and Representatives before mentioned, and the Members of the several State Legislatures, and all executive and judicial Officers, both of the United States and of the several States, shall be bound by Oath or Affirmation, to support this Constitution; but no religious Test shall ever be required as a Qualification to any Office or public Trust under the United States.

US judges are bound by oath to support the Constitution. This is how it is designed to work. First, Congress is not supposed to make any laws that violate the Constitution. There are actually four clauses in the Constitution prohibiting Congress from making any laws outside its limits. Those are in Article 1, Section 8, Paragraph 18.

> To make all Laws which shall be necessary and proper for carrying into Execution the foregoing

> Powers, and all other Powers vested by this
> Constitution in the Government of the United
> States, or in any Department or Officer thereof.

Notice how this clause states powers vested by this Constitution. Vested means authority derived by. This clause is a restraining clause limiting the federal government to only what the Constitution says. However, constitutional scholars claim that this clause actually gives Congress the power to make any law on any subject they deem necessary and proper. They do this by not teaching and ignoring the second half of the clause starting at "vested by."

The other three clauses are Article 3, Section 2, Paragraph 1.

> The judicial Power shall extend to all Cases, in Law
> and Equity, arising under this Constitution, the
> Laws of the United States, and Treaties made, or
> which shall be made, under their Authority.

Again, the phrase "power ... arising under this Constitution" signifies that this is another restraining clause. This time, it specifically restrains the courts.

The third clause that restrains Congress as well as federal and state courts and the executives, the president and governors, is Article 6, Paragraph 2.

> This Constitution, and the Laws of the United
> States which shall be made in Pursuance thereof;
> and all Treaties made, or which shall be made,
> under the Authority of the United States, shall be
> the supreme Law of the Land; and the Judges in
> every State shall be bound thereby, any Thing in the
> Constitution or Laws of any State to the Contrary
> notwithstanding.

Here, all laws and treaties must be in pursuance of the Constitution to be constitutional. Again, a restraining clause. And last, Amendment Ten states,

> The powers not delegated to the United States by the Constitution, nor prohibited by it to the States, are **reserved** to the States respectively, or to the people.

This is quite clear. If a power is not granted to the federal government by this Constitution, it belongs to the states, and the federal government does not have the right or authority to make laws or hear cases regarding those powers.

So back to how the courts gain the power of judicial review. As I mentioned, it is unlawful for Congress to make any laws that are contrary to the Constitution. If it does, the president is supposed to read the law prior to signing it into law and veto it when he discovers it violates the Constitution.

Last, if a law repugnant of the Constitution gets past Congress and the president, and a case is presented in a federal court concerning that law, and the judge realizes the law violates the Constitution, the judge can conduct a judicial review and declare the law unconstitutional. Because of Article 6, Paragraph 3, he is forced to uphold the Constitution, and it is impossible to enforce a law that is in violation of the Constitution when you have taken an oath to support the Constitution.

So judicial review is the means by which the courts uphold the Constitution, but Article 6 grants them the power to review only federal laws that Congress makes. This by no means grants the federal courts the power to review state laws.

So how do courts determine if a federal law is constitutional? Are they just to look at a law and if they don't like it declare it unconstitutional? That is what they are doing today, but is that right? How is it supposed to be done? The first time the Supreme

Court acknowledged its authority to conduct a judicial review was in 1803. Let me give you a quick overview of the case.

Our second president, John Adams, promised to give William Marbury a position as a federal magistrate but never got around to it before his term as president ended. The next president, Thomas Jefferson, selected his friend James Madison as his secretary of state. The job to appoint Marbury as a federal magistrate thus fell to Madison, but Madison did not like Marbury, so he refused. Marbury brought a petition before the Supreme Court and asked the court to issue a writ of mandamus, a court order that requires a government department or official to complete a task.

At that time, the chief justice of the Supreme Court was John Marshall. Marshall reviewed the two laws outlining the courts authority; the Judiciary Act of 1798, and Article 3 of the Constitution. He observed that the law passed by Congress gave the Supreme Court its original authority to issue writs of mandamus in subsection 13;

> The Supreme Court shall also have appellate jurisdiction from the circuit courts and courts of the several states, in the cases herein after provided for' and writs of mandamus ... to any courts appointed, or persons holding office, under the authority of the United States. —Judiciary Act of 1789, ss 13

Marshall then compared it to Article III, the Supreme Court's original authority, and noted no such power had been granted.

> In all Cases affecting Ambassadors, other public Ministers and Consuls, and those in which a State shall be Party, the supreme Court shall have original Jurisdiction. In all the other Cases before mentioned, the Supreme Court shall have appellate Jurisdiction, both as to Law and Fact, with such Exceptions, and

under such Regulations as the Congress shall make.
—Article 3, Section 2, Paragraph 2

Marshall determined that the Constitution and the Judiciary Act conflicted. As you can clearly see as did Marshall, there is no mention of the writ of mandamus in this clause of the Constitution. To get the clearest understanding of how judges are to determine if a federal law is constitutional, read Chief Justice John Marshall's opinion of this case.

> It is empathetically the province and duty of the Judicial Department to say what the law is. Those who apply the rule to particular cases must, of necessity, expound and interpret that rule. If two laws conflict with each other, the Courts must decide on the operation of each.

> So, if a law [e.g., an act, statute, or treaty] be in opposition to the Constitution, if both the law and the Constitution apply to a particular case, so that the Court must either decide that case conformably to the law, disregarding the Constitution, or conformably to the Constitution, disregarding the law. The Court must determine which of these conflicting rules governs the case. This is of the very essence of judicial duty. If, then, the Courts are to regard the Constitution, and the Constitution is superior to any ordinary act of the Legislature, the Constitution, and not such ordinary act, must govern the case to which they both apply.

> Those, then, who controvert the principle that the Constitution is to be considered in court a paramount law are reduced to the necessity of

maintaining that courts must close their eyes on the Constitution, and see only the law.

This doctrine would subvert the very foundation of all written Constitutions.

To what purpose are powers limited, and to what purpose is that limitation committed to writing, if these limits may, at any time, be passed by those intended to be restrained?

Certainly all those who have framed written constitutions contemplate them as forming the fundamental and paramount law of the nation, and consequently, the theory of every such government must be, that an act of the legislature, repugnant to the constitution, is void.

Marshall also stated in his opinion that Congress lacked the power to enlarge or decrease the Supreme Court's original jurisdiction.

Marshall argued that since it was the duty of the courts to determine cases, they have to be able to decide which law applies to each case. Therefore, if two laws conflict with each other, the courts must decide which law applies, and as all judges are sworn to uphold the Constitution, they are forced to apply it. And therefore, the law that was repugnant of the Constitution was declared unconstitutional and no longer had any authority. It is as if the law had never been written.

Do I believe Marshall made the right decision? Absolutely! His reasoning for declaring the Judiciary Act of 1789 unconstitutional is flawless. He was supported by historical documentation such as the Federalist Papers written by Alexander Hamilton, who stated,

The courts were designed to be an intermediate body between the people and the legislature, in order, among other things, *to keep the latter within the limits assigned to their authority.* The interpretation of the laws is the proper and peculiar province of the courts. A constitution is, in fact, and must be regarded by the judges as, a fundamental law. It, therefore, belongs to them to ascertain its meaning, as well as the meaning of any particular act proceeding from the legislative body. If there should happen to be an irreconcilable variance between the two, that which has the superior obligation and validity ought, of course, to be preferred; or, in other words, the Constitution ought to be preferred to the statute, the intention of the people to the intention of their agents.

I am in full agreement with Marshall's decision, but let me throw a monkey wrench into the whole thing by saying that I believe he made the right decision for the wrong thing. He made the assertion that the Constitution did not give the courts the power to issue writs of mandamus. But let's look at Amendment 1 of the Constitution.

Congress shall make no law respecting an establishment of religion, or prohibiting the free exercise thereof; or abridging the freedom of speech, or of the press; or the right of the people peaceably to assemble, and to petition the Government for a redress of grievances.

A redress is meant to rectify or give satisfaction for a wrong. If the government has done a wrong thing to a person and he was awarded restitution, might this imply that the courts have the right to order the government to make good on that restitution? It's the same idea as the Constitution not actually giving the federal courts the power of judicial review, but it is implied under Article 6. A writ of mandamus is not granted specifically, but does not Amendment 1 imply it?

So why do I believe Justice Marshall made the right decision if I believe that the courts were granted if only by implication the power to issue writs of mandamus? We'll go back to the Judiciary Act of 1798.

> The Supreme Court shall also have appellate jurisdiction from the circuit courts and ***courts of the several states***, in the cases herein after provided for' and writs of mandamus ... to any courts appointed, or persons holding office, under the authority of the United States.

Note that it states that the Supreme Court will have the power to hear appeals from state courts. Well, let us, as Marshall did, look at Article 3, but this time at all the authority given to the Supreme Court and lesser courts in Section 2, Paragraphs 1 and 2, and the Eleventh Amendment.

> The judicial Power shall extend to all Cases, in Law and Equity, arising under this Constitution, the Laws of the United States, and Treaties made, or which shall be made, under their Authority; - to all Cases affecting Ambassadors, other public Ministers and Consuls; - to Controversies to which the United States shall be a Party; - to Controversies between two or more States; -{between a State and Citizens of another State;} - between Citizens of different States, - between Citizens of the same state claiming Lands under Grants of different states, {and between a State, or the Citizens thereof, and foreign States, Citizens or Subjects."} —Article 3, Section 2, Paragraph 1

The Judicial power of the United States shall not be construed to extend to any suit in law or equity, commenced or prosecuted against one of United States by Citizens of another State, or by Citizens or Subjects of any Foreign State." —Amendment XI, February 7, 1795

I put Amendment Eleven right after paragraph 1 so you could see that everything in brackets was repealed by the amendment giving the Supreme Court even less authority than it originally had. Now read paragraph 2.

In all Cases affecting Ambassadors, other public Ministers and Consuls, and those in which a State shall be Party, the supreme Court shall have original Jurisdiction. In all the other Cases before mentioned, the Supreme Court shall have appellate Jurisdiction, both as to Law and Fact, with such Exceptions, and under such Regulations as the Congress shall make. —Article 3, Section 2, Paragraph 2

This is it. This is absolutely all the authority given to the Supreme Court and lesser courts and no more. Look real hard; see if you can find where it grants the federal courts the power to hear appeals from state courts. You can't, can you? That is because it's not there. They can hear cases where there is a dispute between two or more states, and they can hear cases when they are being sued by the states. But nowhere can it be found that they can hear appeals from state court cases. (That is any case that state courts have original jurisdiction over.) So the Judiciary Act of 1798 and any other act of Congress that allows the Supreme Court or lesser courts to hear appeals from the state courts is repugnant of the Constitution (Article 3, Sections 1 and 2, and the Eleventh Amendment) and is therefore void. Thus, Chief Justice Marshall made the right decision but for the wrong reason.

So now you know exactly how to determine if a law is constitutional and how a judge is to determine if a law is, or is not constitutional—by holding the law in question up to the Constitution. If the law is in agreement with the Constitution, it is constitutional, but if it is not in agreement, then and only then is it unconstitutional and therefore void. A judge cannot declare a law unconstitutional just because he feels it is inappropriate. That is not his call.

Another fact that goes unnoticed in our scholarly society is the fact that Article 6, Paragraph 3 requires the governors, the legislatures, and the judges of the states to take the same oath to support the Constitution as does the president, members of Congress, and federal judges. This implies that they too can determine and declare an act of Congress unconstitutional as well. Think about it. If they enforce an unconstitutional and therefore an unlawful act, they violate their oath to support the Constitution. So what the founding fathers did was make state governments the last line of defense against unconstitutional and thus unlawful laws coming out of the nation's capital.

I will discuss in my next article what our founders wanted for us in terms of the fourth branch of government. Remember how I stated in my first article that the first time around in the federal police academy in 1991 we were taught about the four branches of government outlined in the Constitution. You guessed it, the fourth of course is the State government.

CHAPTER THREE

ARTICLES 4-5

Article 4: The Rights of the States Part 1

The driving force behind the intent of the founding fathers when they established this nation and the Constitution was their overwhelming desire to be a free people. They wrote the Constitution in a manner that would allow the people to always maintain the most control. The only way for the people to maintain their freedom is by ensuring they can always have the ultimate power over the government. To that end, they must divide and limit power. This is what the Constitution does.

To which government did our founders give the greatest amount of authority and responsibility? Did they make state governments subject to the federal government, or did they make the federal government subject to state governments? When you study the Constitution, it becomes obvious that the founders wanted to make the states dominant over the federal government. Anyone shocked by this statement? The Constitution makes it clear that the states are the dominant government and that the federal government is to play second fiddle.

But what is taught in our public schools, colleges, and universities?

The fact that you are probably in doubt about how true a statement this is is evidence of what you have been taught. Regardless, my statement is all too easy to prove.

Remember in my second article, *A Look at a Constitutional Republic, What our Founders Were Looking For,* when I introduced you to Robert Natelson? He was the constitutional law professor at the University of Montana. He had given a presentation on the Constitution for a Tea Party town hall meeting in 2009. At one point in his presentation, he stated that he did not care for the term *states' rights*. He stated, "The founding fathers did not establish enumerated powers and rights in the Constitution for the prerogative of the States, but for the liberty of the people." The entire Constitution is designed to secure the freedom and liberty of the people; that is its primary purpose. Our founding fathers were very intelligent men, and just as you and I have rights and corporations have rights, state governments have rights that go hand in hand with their power and authority. This our founding fathers clearly understood. So why this uneducation from Natelson? Notice that it leaves in the mind of the listener the idea that the state has less significance and therefore less authority than it actually has.

Many things Natelson said in his presentation contradicted what I learned about the Constitution. Through the rest of these articles, I will be addressing some of the statements he made I know to be untrue. I do not believe Natelson is nefarious—absolutely not. I have listened to his entire presentation and his beliefs, and I believe he is a man of integrity but a product of modern scholastic teachings, a victim of academia. Bad teaching leads to more bad teaching. So when he made the comment that the founders did not spell out the enumerated powers of the states for the benefit of the states, I felt inclined to test him.

I asked him what his perception was of Article 4 of the Constitution in regard to its giving the states full faith and credit concerning public acts and how that would affect Obamacare. He read Article 4, Section 1 and then gave a definition for judicial proceedings. To paraphrase, he said, "If a court in one state renders a judgment against a person so as to be required to pay restitution for alimony or child support and the like and the person with the decree against him flees to another state, the state the person fled to is required to enforce the decree of the court of the state the subject fled from."

He said,

> If a person is married in one state it is to be recognize in another state. Now the state of Massachusetts has made a law recognizing same sex marriages. Does this mean that under the judicial proceeding clause other States have to recognize same sex marriages as well?

He talked about a law Congress made stating that no, other states don't have to. Last, he stated that Article 4 really had no big overarching significance other than in regard to marriage and that it was mainly a housekeeping issue.

Okay, this is an example of what I am talking about bad teaching (uneducation). And this is taught and believed at every level of academia in America. How true it is when the Bible states in Proverbs 18:17 (NIV): "The first to present his case seems right, till another comes forward and questions him." Notice how he marginalized this article: "No big overarching significance and merely a housekeeping issue." Let's analyze this whole article and see if our scholar was telling the truth.

Full Faith and Credit shall be given in each State to the public Acts, Records, and judicial Proceedings of every other State. And the Congress may by general Laws prescribe the Manner in which such Acts, Records and Proceedings shall be proved, and the Effect thereof. —Article 4, Section 1

Notice how this article starts out: "Full Faith and Credit." This is not a vernacular we use a lot today, so how would we say the same thing today? We would say all authority; full faith and credit and all authority mean the same. I also want you to look at the words *faith, credit, acts, records,* and *proceedings* in the article above. Notice they are all capitalized. They are not proper nouns, and they are not at the start of the sentence. That is how they are written in the Constitution. In 1787, they did not have **bold,** or *italics,* or <u>underscore,</u> so when the founders wanted to emphasize the importance of something, they capitalized the first letter.

So do you think by the fact that our founding fathers are about to bestow upon someone or something all authority and by the fact that they were trying to emphasize it that it might be important? With just these two facts, I feel pretty safe in saying that we can throw Natelson's statement about Article 4 having no big, overarching significance and merely a housekeeping issue right out the door.

I want to point out a big mistake made by modern constitutional law professors. They mistakenly claim that this clause in the Constitution has the same meaning as Article 4, paragraph 3, in the Articles of Confederation. The aforementioned explanation given by Natelson does apply to this paragraph, but does it apply to Article 4 of the Constitution? Let's look at the two clauses side by side and see if you notice the difference.

Articles of Confederation, Article 4, Paragraph 3	US Constitution, Article 4, Section 1
Full faith and credit shall be given in each of these states to the records, acts, and judicial proceedings of the courts and magistrates of every other state.	Full Faith and Credit shall be given in each State to the public Acts, Records, and judicial Proceedings of every other State.

Notice the difference? It is the word *public* before the word *acts.* This word changes the entire scope of the implied authority given.

So just how significant is Article 4? Let's continue to analyze it and see.

We see that all authority (full faith and credit) is being given to the states, so we know that it is state governments we're talking about when we look at the type of authority our founding fathers bestowed. The first power they bestowed on the states was for public acts. Acts, as our founding fathers knew them, are defined as

> the result of public deliberation, or the decision of a prince, legislative body, council, court of justice or magistrate; a decree, edict, law, judgment, resolve, award, determination; as an act of parliament, or of congress, The term is also transferred to the book, record, or writing, containing the laws and determinations. - *American Dictionary of The English Language*, Noah Webster, 1828

Public acts are all laws and regulations dealing with the public—you and I, the people. Would education be a public act? Yes. According to this article, who has all authority to make laws governing education? The states. How much of this authority is retained by the federal government? None. The federal government has no authority to make any laws concerning education. Would work be a public act? Yes. According to this article, the states have all authority to make labor laws; the federal government has no authority to make labor laws. Would health care be a public act? Yes. Health care legislation is a public act vested in the states, not the federal government. The federal government no authority to make such laws.

I think you're getting the meaning of the first power granted to the states, so let's move to the second power granted the states by this article.

I wrote in my second article that all you needed to understand the Constitution was an eighth-grade education and the ability to think. Let's apply our eighth-grade English and see what the comma after acts means. The comma signifies that we're talking about the same topic (in this case public) but are addressing a different subject (in this case Records). So the second power of the states granted by this article is public records. It is the states' authority to keep all public records such as birth certificates, marriage certificates, titles and deeds to land, and all forms of identification such as driver's licenses and ID cards—anything regarding the people and where a public record of it is kept.

A few years back, the federal government tried to pass a bill requiring all Americans to have a federal driver's license. The states finally showed some backbone and refused to let the law pass as it was clearly infringing on their right to keep public records. As the federal government did not have a leg to stand on, it backed off, and the bill was never passed.

Now, the federal government is trying to force the public to obtain the Real ID, a federal ID for Americans to allow them into federal buildings and to fly on aircraft. Our federal government has no more authority to demand this ID than it did to demand we have a federal driver's license. Both records violate this clause of Article 4 and are unconstitutional. The Real ID violates Article 4 and Amendment 14, Section 1 as well: "All persons born or naturalized in the United States, and subject to the jurisdiction thereof, are citizens of the United States and **of the State wherein they reside.**"

What this clause is stating is that a person born in a state is a citizen of that state and a citizen of the United States at the same time. You can't be one without being the other. And as only state governments may issue an ID card as it is a public record and states can issue only its citizens these ID cards or driver's licenses, the federal government is forced by both Article 4 and the Fourteenth Amendment to recognize these state-issued forms as proof a citizenship. This makes the Real ID card unconstitutional, and an exercise of futility. So why the desire of the federal government to make all Americans have the Real ID? I'll address this in my last article. I promise, you won't like the answer.

How about income tax filings and Social Security numbers (sometimes referred to as tax identification numbers)? Would they fall under the states' authority under the Constitution to keep all public records? The Sixteenth Amendment gives Congress the power to lay and collect taxes on income, but this is all the amendment allows Congress to do. It in no way implies that Congress or the federal government can keep any records of those income tax filings. So a law that would be in compliance with the Constitution would require the states to issue tax IDs or SSNs and keep all the tax records on file as well. The states would collect all the income revenues for the federal government and hand them over to it. That is all that is required to fulfill the Sixteenth Amendment. The way the tax laws are written now are repugnant of the Constitution and therefore unlawful, unconstitutional, and void. Does this sound insignificant to you?

How do I know that my interpretation of Article 4 is the correct interpretation, and all the modern scholars have it wrong? Easy. Madison clearly stated this in the Federalist Papers, Article 45, *The Alleged Danger From the Powers of the Union to the State Governments Considered.*

> The powers delegated by the proposed Constitution to the federal government are few and defined. Those which are to remain in the State governments are numerous and indefinite. The former will be exercised principally on external objects, as war, peace, negotiation, and foreign commerce; with which last the power of taxation will, for the most part, be connected. The powers reserved to the several States will extend to all the objects which, in the ordinary course of affairs, concern the lives, liberties, and properties of the people, and the internal order, improvement, and prosperity of the State. The operations of the federal government will be most extensive and important in times of war and danger; those of the State governments, in times of peace and security.

Article 4, Section 1 is the only clause that secures these powers for the states.

I think you're beginning to see that the power behind the right to keep public records is solely a state right, so let's move on to judicial proceedings.

Natelson started with a good explanation of judicial proceedings but then blew it. If you are taken to a civil court for let's say divorce or maybe you caused damage to someone's property or have failed to keep your part of a bargain and the judge renders a judgment against you requiring you to pay alimony or child support or restitution for the damage you caused, this clause applies. Let's say the civil proceeding was in Nevada and you move to Utah to escape paying the alimony, child support, or restitution. It won't work because every state in this union is required by this clause to enforce the decree of the court of any other state. So Utah would ensure you paid your alimony or child support or whatever form of restitution you are required to make.

This and only this is what this clause is requiring of the states. But Natelson went on to talk about a law in Massachusetts regarding same-sex marriage and a federal judge declaring that law constitutional. Does any of this apply to this clause? Marriage is a holy sacrament ordained by God (Genesis 2:24). This ordinance is well over three thousand years old. You may be married by a priest, pastor, ship's captain, or anyone else licensed to preform marriages such as a magistrate. It is not a judgment; it is a ceremony, and it is a free choice between a man and a woman. No judge says, "I hereby sentence you to life with this man, and you to life with this woman." Even if a federal judge declares a law constitutional (If a federal judge actually has that authority. That we'll look at later), he is only stating his opinion; it is the opinion of the court that the law is constitutional. No judgment as applied in this clause has been rendered. And this clause is not concerned about laws. Laws are covered in Section 2 of this article. The letter of this law is clear here, and in no way can the spirit of the law be used to infer that all states are bound by that opinion because the connotations of the spirit of a law must always be found in the letter of the law. There is no such inference here.

Also, the spirit of the law is never ludicrous, and it is ludicrous to believe that the opinion of one man or a panel of nine could supersede the sovereignty of a state. Hopefully, this is all clear, so let's move on to the second clause of Section 1 covering general laws.

> And the Congress may by general Laws prescribe the Manner in which such Acts, Records and Proceedings shall be proved, and the Effect thereof.
> —Article 4, Section 1, Second Clause.

Notice that is says "may." This means that it is not mandatory; Congress doesn't have to make any such laws. But if it feels compelled to because a circumstance arises requiring a public act to be addressed, it can pass a general law, meaning the law is not specific in nature and does not outline details as they feel a law should look like, and the law can only ask a state to prove that a certain law exists and ascertain how effective that law or laws are. That's it. This clause does not give Congress the authority to make laws governing a public act binding upon the states. Civil rights acts are in violation of this clause; they are not supported by this clause. In the 1850s, civil right acts were struck down by the Supreme Court as unconstitutional being in violation of this clause.

A general law that would be constitutional under this clause would be no longer than three paragraphs long and would look and sound something like this.

> Patence of nobility should be given.

> In accordance with Article 4, Section 1 and in compliance with that same section; Congress has recognized the fact that the cost of health care

has risen to excessive and in many cases for most citizens within the United States, even crippling rates. Congress also recognizes the fact that the good health of its citizens is intertwined with the health of this nation as a whole, and that there need be laws in place that allow all the citizens of the several states to obtain health care that would not impose financial struggles.

Therefore, this Congress is requiring each state of this union to present the laws that it has enacted concerning health care in general and specifically how these laws make health care affordable to all of its citizenry. At the same time each state shall prove by a statistical report how many of their citizens are taking advantage of these laws and how their financial burden has been reduced.

This proof shall be presented before a congressional committee the next time the Congress shall convene.

Notice that the first thing I do is give what I call a patence of nobility of the law, meaning I show where the law derives its authority from and I list any clauses in the Constitution that convey limitations or immunities. It is my belief that any law in the United States whether federal, state, county, or municipal should start out with a patence of nobility. I'll explain later.

Next, still in the first paragraph, I convey Congress's concern and what public act it is concerned about (health care and primarily its being affordable). In the next paragraph, Congress gives the command that the states present the laws they have enacted in regard to health care or whatever public act they are concerned about, and it gives a means by which the states can prove the effectiveness of their laws.

In my example, I used a statistical report, but they could have chosen to use auditors or conducted a poll of the citizens of the state to see how effective they felt the laws were. All three are legitimate ways for the federal government to ascertain the effectiveness of a state's laws under Article 4, Section 1.

The last thing needed is for the act to state to whom the states will present this information to and when such as given in paragraph 3. This is all a constitutional law under the general law clause would look like.

The Affordable Care Act is well over 2,000 pages long and micromanages every aspect of health care. In the previous article, I wrote about how to determine if a law is constitutional. By applying that test, you can see that this act is repugnant of the general laws clause of Article 4 and the public acts clause of Article 4 as well. This is just for starters. It also violates Article 1, Section 8, and the Tenth Amendment. Obamacare is an unlawful act and is invalid or void.

Natelson said that all of Article 4 was insignificant and merely a housekeeping issue. So in my next article, I will address the rest of Article 4, Sections 2–4 and see if our scholar is being truthful with us.

Article 5: The Rights of the States Part 2

In part one of "The Rights of the States," we looked at Article 4, Section 1. I mentioned earlier that Natelson did not care for the term *states' rights*. His claim was that the enumerated powers in the Constitution were not put there for the states but for the liberty of the people. I then made a case showing that our founding fathers had enumerated the states' rights very much so for the benefit of the states, and I just covered Section 1 of Article 4. Yet Natelson stated that all of Article 4 had no big overarching significance and was merely a housekeeping issue. Let's look at the rest of Article 4 and determine if our scholar is being scholarly. Does the rest of Article 4 have any overarching significance? Here is the rest of Article 4.

Section 2. The Citizens of each State shall be entitled to all Privileges and Immunities of Citizens in the several States.

A Person charged in any State with Treason, Felony, or other Crime, who shall flee from Justice, and be found in another State, shall on Demand of the executive Authority of the State from which he fled, be delivered up, to be removed to the State having Jurisdiction of the Crime.

{No Person held to Service or Labour in one State, under the Laws thereof, escaping into another, shall, in Consequence of any Law or Regulation therein, be discharged from such Service or Labour, but shall be delivered up on Claim of the Party to whom such Service or Labour may be due. Repealed by Amendment XIII}

Section 3. New States may be admitted by the Congress into this Union; but no new State shall be formed or erected within the Jurisdiction of any other State; nor any State be formed by the Junction of two or more States, or Parts of States, without the Consent of the Legislatures of the States concerned as well as of the Congress.

The Congress shall have Power to dispose of and make all needful Rules and Regulations respecting the Territory or other Property belonging to the United States; and nothing in this Constitution shall be so construed as to Prejudice any Claims of the United States, or of any particular State.

> **Section 4.** The United States shall guarantee to every State in this Union a Republican Form of Government, and shall protect each of them against Invasion; and on Application of the Legislature, or of the Executive (when the Legislature cannot be convened), against domestic Violence. —Article 4

Let's break this article down and look at each section and paragraph separately. The first paragraph of Section 2 states, "The Citizens of each State shall be entitled to all Privileges and Immunities of Citizens in the several States." This means exactly what it says. Let me use the law Massachusetts made concerning same-sex marriages as an example. Privileges and immunities in this clause refer to what we normally call rights today. In the Constitution, we would call the first ten amendments and Article 1, Sections 9 and 10 rights, but they would have been listed as privileges and immunities by our founders.

The privilege Massachusetts granted by law was same-sex marriages. The Massachusetts legislation can do this because it is dealing with the public, and this clause acknowledges the power of the states to grant privileges. I consider this a significant state right, but according to our scholar, this is mere housekeeping. Anyway, Massachusetts granted same-sex marriages by law. This is a privilege. Immunities in this clause means that no county or municipal government in Massachusetts can pass any law or hear any civil or criminal court case that would abridge this privilege protected by the state's law. It is—you got it—immune. As county and municipal governments derive their authority from the state, they and any law they make are subject to state laws.

Does this mean that other states now have to acknowledge same-sex marriages? No! All we need to do is skip on down to Section 4 of this article to determine that. Section 4 states, "The United States shall guarantee to every State in this Union a Republican Form of Government." This means that each state in the union is its own sovereignty; it is independent of the US government and other state governments. Take a look at Federalist Papers 40 and 45 as proof of that. The relationship between state governments and the federal government is purely symbiotic. The states are sovereign but are essential for the working of the union and federal government; no law made by one state can be forced on any other state. Each state can make laws only for itself, and no federal judge has the authority to say otherwise.

Section 2, Paragraph 1 states that the citizens of each state shall be entitled to all privileges and immunities of citizens in the several states. Using our Massachusetts example again, if a homosexual couple in Colorado goes to Massachusetts and applies for a marriage license, neither Massachusetts nor any of its counties or city governments can say to the couple, "Sorry, this law and privilege is only for citizens of Massachusetts. You're from Colorado, so take a hike." Massachusetts can't do that. This clause guarantees that citizens from every state can go to Massachusetts to take advantage of the privilege; Massachusetts cannot deny them. It binds only the state granting the privilege. If the homosexual couple goes back to Colorado, Colorado does not have to recognize their Massachusetts marriage; it all depends on that sovereign state's laws. Again, no federal judge or judges have the authority over the sovereignty of the state.

Paragraph 2 of Section 2 states,

> A Person charged in any State with Treason, Felony, or other Crime, who shall flee from Justice, and be found in another State, shall on Demand of the executive Authority of the State from which he fled, be delivered up, to be removed to the State having Jurisdiction of the Crime.

This is extradition. This is a right of a state, not a private right, and it is not talking about the liberty of the person; it is talking about the incarceration of the person. This would seem to contradict what Natelson had to say about states' rights.

Paragraph 3 of Section 2 states,

> No Person held to Service or Labour in one State,
> under the Laws thereof, escaping into another, shall,
> in Consequence of any Law or Regulation therein,
> be discharged from such Service or Labour, but
> shall be delivered up on Claim of the Party to whom
> such Service or Labour may be due.

This paragraph is talking about slavery and was repealed by
Amendment 13, so it no longer has standing.

Section 3, Paragraph 1 states,

> New States may be admitted by the Congress into
> this Union; but no new State shall be formed or
> erected within the Jurisdiction of any other State;
> nor any State be formed by the Junction of two or
> more States, or Parts of States, without the Consent
> of the Legislatures of the States concerned as well
> as of the Congress.

Let's say the citizens of northern California get sick and tired
of the ridiculous laws coming out of the legislature of the southern
part of the state and decide to invoke their individual liberty and
make a new state out of the northern half of California. Can they
do it? No. As you can see in this clause, the state has full authority
to say what goes on with the property in its borders. This seems to
me as a rather substantial states' right, which again defies what our
scholar had to say.

Paragraph 2 of Section 3 states,

> The Congress shall have Power to dispose of and
> make all needful Rules and Regulations respecting
> the Territory or other Property belonging to the

United States, and nothing in this Constitution shall be so construed as to Prejudice any Claims of the United States, or of any particular State.

The property of the US talked about here includes military installations, arsenals, dockyards, post offices, mints, federal courthouses, etc. Territories laid claim by the US government today consist of islands such as Guam, Puerto Rico, the Virgin Islands, and a couple others out there. This clause gives Congress the right to make any laws it deems necessary and proper even over public acts in these territories or needful buildings. It is the US government's property.

Now what does "Claims ... of any particular State" mean? The two best examples I can give you are found in Florida and Alaska. Florida has claim to the Florida Keys, a group of islands at its southern tip. Florida has full authority over these islands. It can make any law it deems necessary for these islands or do what it will with these islands, and it is solely up to Florida. The US government has no authority over these islands. It is no concern of the federal government what Florida does with these islands at all. The same is true for the Alaska Aleutian chain of islands. These islands are the claim of Alaska, which has full authority over them to do as it will. Again, the US government has no authority over these islands and has no say about what Alaska does with them. The islands are the property of the state.

We kind of looked at Section 4 already, and as I mentioned, the US guarantees each state its own sovereign republic. It also guarantees that if a state is invaded by a foreign nation, the US will protect it. If Mexico were to invade Nevada, the US government would jump in and assist Nevada in kicking Mexico's tail and send them packing back to Mexico. The US government does not have to ask permission of the state to do this; it is required of it. But if there is an outbreak of domestic violence in a state, the state can handle the violence any way it deems proper including calling up the Army and Air National Guard to squash the outbreak. The state does not have to ask permission of Congress, the president, or the Supreme Court and is not accountable to them. Because of this clause, the federal government cannot get involved unless the state petitions it by an application. This is the power of the state or states' right.

So how do Sections 3 and 4 of Article 4 work in a practical application? Let us say the territory of Guam petitions Congress for statehood and Congress admits Guam as a state. At that time, the US government relinquishes all its authority over that property, and none of the laws and regulations governing Guam while it was the property of the US are valid. Guam becomes its own sovereignty and will make all the laws it deems necessary for governing its people. And if there are any other islands around Guam that Guam laid claim to, it has full authority over them as well.

This is an incredible amount of authority and a great amount of rights the states have. This is totally opposite of what Natelson was teaching, and we have only scratched the top layer of the authority the Constitution gives the states.

Have you noticed how nowadays there always seems to be a US court declaring a state law constitutional or not? Do the US courts have the authority to review a state law and decide if it is lawful? What does the Constitution say?

We looked at Article 1, Section 8, Paragraph 18 in my third article.

> ... to make all Laws which shall be necessary and proper for carrying into Execution the foregoing Powers, and all other Powers vested by this Constitution in the Government of the United States, or in any Department or Officer thereof.

Notice how it states that all powers of officers of the US government are vested by the Constitution. This means that for an officer of the US government to have power—and all US judges are officers of the US—that power must be granted by the Constitution.

If it can't be found in the Constitution, it doesn't exist. Simple, right? When a judge looks at a law to determine if it is constitutional or not, this is called judicial review. Judicial review is the doctrine under which legislative and executive actions are subject to review and possible invalidation by the judiciary. So we would have to look at the entire Constitution to determine if a federal judge has the authority to conduct a judicial review of a state law.

Sometimes, you hear scholars and politicians state something like, "The Bill of Rights is not applicable to treaties" as if the Bill of Rights and the Constitution were different documents. Let me illuminate you; there is no Bill of Rights. The Bill of Rights was a nickname given to the first ten amendments that were ratified in 1791. The key term here is *ratified*. This means that the proposed bill was made into law and is no longer a bill. And when a proposed amendment is ratified, it becomes part of the Constitution just as the original seven articles are. We see this in Article 5 where it states, "… shall be valid to all Intents and Purposes, as Part of this Constitution, when ratified by the Legislatures of three fourths of the several States, or by Conventions in three fourths thereof."

Amendment 1 is every bit a part of the Constitution as Article 1 or any of the other original articles are. So are all the rest of the amendments from the First to the Twenty-Seventh. Anyone who tells you that a law or treaty of the United States or a state does not have to apply to the Bill of Rights is lying. Right now, the Bill of Rights is just a name to reference the first ten amendments ratified. They are the Constitution.

So when we want to look to see if a US judge has the authority to conduct a judicial review of a state law, we have to look at the entire Constitution, from Article 1 to Amendment Twenty-Seven, to see if that power is granted. As we found out in my third article, Congress lacks the power to give the judicial branch any additional power by mere laws, so we can look only to the Constitution for that power. Is there anywhere in the Constitution that talks about the power of judicial review of state laws? Yes. Article 6, Paragraph 2.

> This Constitution, and the Laws of the United
> States which shall be made in Pursuance thereof;
> and all Treaties made, or which shall be made,
> under the Authority of the United States, shall be
> the supreme Law of the Land; **and the <u>Judges in</u>**
> **<u>every State</u> shall be bound thereby, any Thing**
> **in the Constitution or Laws of any State to the**
> **Contrary notwithstanding**.

Notice how this clause starts with the laws of the United States, which shall be made in pursuance of the Constitution. This clause restrains the federal government. What this signifies is that for a law enacted by Congress to be constitutional and legal, there must be verbiage in the Constitution that allows that law to be made. Remember when I stated that I believed all laws at all levels of government should have patence of nobility? This is why.

Next, it states that treaties must be made under the authority of the United States. What is the authority of the United States? The Constitution! Again, no treaty can be made if it is not in compliance with the Constitution. If a treaty violates any portion to the Constitution, it is useless and unenforceable. Again, if there was a patence of nobility, this would simplify matters greatly.

Next, it states that the Constitution and laws and treaties made under the Constitution are the supreme law of the land. That means that every law written in the United States including state, county, municipal, and yes, even HOA - Home Owner Association- laws, must be in compliance with the Constitution. All laws and jurisdictions are subject to it. This is easily ascertained by the next clause, the one we came to examine. This clause requires judicial review of state laws and state constitutions. But the real question is, does it allow US courts to conduct judicial review of state laws? It states, "… and the Judges in every State shall be bound thereby, any Thing in the Constitution or Laws of any State to the Contrary notwithstanding."

It talks about the judges in every state, meaning state judges. Does it say anything about the US Supreme Court? No. Does it say anything about any form of federal courts? No. It specifically singles out state judges, and it is all inclusive, meaning the state supreme court, state appellate courts, the state district courts, and municipal magistrates. As all laws are subject to the Constitution, all the levels of state judges are required to review every law made in the state, county, and cities to ensure they are in compliance with the Constitution and all legal federal laws.

I emphasize the word *legal.* States do not have to comply with any law passed by Congress, any US court order, or any executive order by the president if those laws, opinions, or executive orders are unconstitutional and therefore illegal. Not only do they not have to; they are required under oath not to enforce any unlawful action of the federal government. Article 6, Paragraph 3 requires state governors, legislatures, and judiciaries to take oaths to support the Constitution. This is the clause from which the Supreme Court derives its authority to conduct judicial reviews of all laws coming out of Congress, federal laws. So all state officers have the same authority that the Supreme Court has to determine if a law coming out of Congress is constitutional. If it is not, the states must ignore that law. There is no way you can support the Constitution and enforce a law that violates it at the same time. Can't happen.

When I gave my presentation on the Constitution at a Tea Party meeting in 2016 and showed this clause to the audience, someone asked, "If a federal judge is in the state, wouldn't this clause apply to him?" There are five reasons we can eliminate the idea that this clause would apply to federal judges just because they presided in a certain state. First, there was no original intent to set up district judges; instead, circuit judges were established. Second, it is a matter of jurisdiction. Third, it is a violation of the states' sovereignty under Article 4, Section 4. Fourth, it violates Article 3, Section 2. Last, it is clear by the structure of this clause that it is specifically addressing the state.

We need to look at the history behind this clause. At the time of its writing, there were no federal district judges and no intent to establish them. There was the Supreme Court, but it convened in the District of Columbia, so it was on federal property, not state property. It is not a matter of presence; it is a matter of jurisdiction. (This is true for present-day district judges. Federal courthouses are islands of federal property in the states but not parts of the states.) Then instead of having district judges as we have today, our founders went with circuit judges who traveled across all the states to hear cases but only those involving federal jurisdiction.

This is the third reason we can eliminate the idea that this clause applies to federal judges just because they preside in states. Each state is sovereign, and a federal judge has no part of that sovereignty. This sovereignty is guaranteed under Article 4, Section 4 of the Constitution.

Last, federal judges are not given any authority in Article 3 of the Constitution to do so. The list of jurisdiction is spelled out very clearly in Article 3, and the federal government, especially the courts, is not given any authority over state matters except for disputes between states and disputes between states and the federal government. So we see that Article 6, Paragraph 2 gives state judges authority to conduct judicial review of state laws but does not give this authority to federal judges.

Is there any other clause in the Constitution that might allow a federal justice to conduct a judicial review of a state law? No, and there wouldn't be. Think about it. If there was such a clause, wouldn't it contradict Article 4, Section 4 that makes a state sovereign? Yes, it would. And unlike our leaders today, our founding fathers were actually intelligent men. They wouldn't have made such a mindless mistake. Therefore, no federal judge, whether a Supreme Court justice or a federal magistrate, has the authority or legal right to conduct a judicial review of any state law. It is not in their jurisdiction, and doing so would violate the Constitution and be a criminal act. All rulings ever made by federal judges in this regard are invalid and therefore unenforceable. The state governments can merely ignore the opinions.

Who is dominant, the guy asking for more power or the guy granting more power? It's the guy who can grant power. This is exactly what Article 5 of the Constitution does for the state. Congress can introduce an amendment but it is the states that must ratify it. The states also can introduce and ratify amendments to the Constitution granting more power to or reducing the power of the federal government. This clearly demonstrates that the founding fathers intended to make the states dominant over the US government.

How do I know that all the scholars and politicians have it wrong and I have it right? Easy. The men who wrote the Constitution left nothing to chance; they spelled everything out. It is quite clear in Federalist Paper 45, in which Madison wrote this.

> The powers delegated by the proposed Constitution to the federal government are few and defined. Those which are to remain in the State governments are numerous and indefinite. The former will be exercised principally on external objects, as war, peace, negotiation, and foreign commerce; with which last the power of taxation will, for the most part, be connected. The powers reserved to the several States will extend to all the objects which, in the ordinary course of affairs, concern the lives, liberties, and properties of the people, and the internal order, improvement, and prosperity of the State. The operations of the federal government will be most extensive and important in times of war and danger; those of the State governments, in times of peace and security.

Can it get any clearer than this? Article 4 delegates that authority to the states. Only state governments are responsible for the well-being of the people.

The last proof I would like to give showing that the founding fathers intended the states be the dominant authority in the US is the Tenth Amendment: "The powers not delegated to the United States, nor prohibited to the States, are **reserved [exclusive to]** to the States or to the People." This is of course another restraining clause; it is saying that if there is not a clause in the Constitution granting the federal government a certain power, that power belongs to the state governments or the people. If it isn't spelled out in the Constitution, the federal government cannot do it. But you will be amazed at how the federal government misspells and misinterprets the Constitution. In my thirteenth article, I will go into greater detail as to how Congress and the federal courts justify ignoring the Tenth Amendment.

This is why I can make the assertions that the dominant governing body is the states and that the US government is subordinate to them.

So far, we have looked at the rights or authority of the states and the limitations of the US courts. Shortly, I think it will be good to look at the limitations of the presidency and Congress. I think I'll name those articles "Shortcomings."

—March 17, 2015

CORRUPTION OF THE JUDICIARY

(This was originally my fifth script for the YouTube videos I had hoped to make of "Our Constitution Made Easy." You'll see why I added it to this chapter.)

When people today think of the Supreme Court, they think of it as the branch of the federal government with the ultimate power, supreme. No! The word *supreme* in Supreme Court merely means it is the highest court in the federal court system, nothing more. Actually, it is the weakest branch of the government outlined in the Constitution. But the Constitution holds it to the highest standards.

This is why the criminal activity it has perpetrated makes it the vilest of the branches of government. Let's look at what limited authority has been given them. Their powers are enumerated in Article 3.

> The judicial Power of the United States shall be vested in one supreme Court, and in such inferior Courts as the Congress may from time to time ordain and establish. The Judges, both of the supreme and inferior Courts, shall hold their Offices during good Behaviour, and shall, at stated Times, receive for their Services a Compensation, which shall not be diminished during their Continuance in Office. —Article 3, Section 1

I didn't misspell behavior; that's the original spelling, but notice that it states that a judge will hold his office during good behavior. Most scholars will tell you that this is a life appointment that is next to impossible to remove someone from. It's true that this clause gives the judge the opportunity to live out his life as a judge, but this clause is intended to elevate the standard of the judge making it easier for his removal for misbehavior.

Article 2 Section. 4 states,

> The President, Vice President and all civil Officers [this includes judges and congressmen of the United States,] shall be removed from Office on Impeachment for, and Conviction of, Treason, Bribery, or other high Crimes and Misdemeanors. High crimes are felonies.

Yes, committing any of these crimes constitutes bad behavior, but when you look at the historical reasons for the thirteen judges who have been impeached here in the US, you find one was impeached for cussing in his courtroom and another for public intoxication.

Neither was a crime, but they were definitely not good behavior. As you can see through the lens of history, judges are to be held to a higher standard. It's the nature of their business. They are judging others, so their character needs to be exemplary. Let's move on. Section 2 states,

> The judicial Power shall extend to all Cases, in Law and Equity, arising under this Constitution, the Laws of the United States, and Treaties made, or which shall be made, under their Authority; [This is the fourth restrictive clause I talked about in my third video, congressional abuses, Notice it limits the judicial power to laws **arising under** the constitution. All laws and treaties have to be in compliance with the constitution to be constitutional.] '1). --to all Cases affecting Ambassadors, other public Ministers and Consuls; 2).--to all Cases of admiralty and maritime Jurisdiction; 3).--to Controversies to which the United States shall be a Party; 4). --to Controversies between two or more States; 5).-- between a State and Citizens of another State; 6).--between Citizens of different States; 7). --between Citizens of the same State claiming Lands under Grants of different States, and 8). between a State, or the Citizens thereof, and foreign States, Citizens or Subjects.

Amendment XI, passed by Congress March 4, 1794 and ratified February 7, 1795.

> The Judicial power of the United States shall not be construed to extend to any suit in law or equity, commenced or prosecuted against one of the United

States by Citizens of another State, or by Citizens or Subjects of any Foreign State.

That leaves six subjects that the federal courts can hear cases on—six! Any case involving any other matter is a crime for them to hear. They cannot do it. No act of Congress can enlarge or decrease the authority of the courts; only an amendment can do that, and there has never been an amendment that has increased their authority.

> In all Cases affecting Ambassadors, other public Ministers and Consuls, and those in which a State shall be Party, the supreme Court shall have original Jurisdiction. In all the other Cases before mentioned, the supreme Court shall have appellate Jurisdiction, both as to Law and Fact, with such Exceptions, and under such Regulations as the Congress shall make.

This portion is the sixth and final check and balance placed in the Constitution. The Seventeenth Amendment voided the Seventh check and balance.

That's it! This is the extent of the powers of the Supreme Court and the inferior courts. There's not much here, is there? Let me go over each of these powers again and I'll give you a brief explanation of each.

1. To all Cases affecting Ambassadors, other public Ministers and Consuls. This clause allows the Supreme Court to hear cases involving international laws. It also allows it to have primary jurisdiction in cases where an ambassador is involved.
2. To all Cases of admiralty and maritime Jurisdiction. If a crime is committed on the high seas or other bodies of water, the federal government has jurisdiction.

3. To Controversies to which the United States shall be a Party. If a state or even a private party sued the federal government, the Supreme Court would try the case.
4. To Controversies between two or more States. This clause and the sixth clause are pretty much self-explanatory.
6. Between Citizens of different States
7. Between Citizens of the same State claiming Lands under Grants of different States. This clause had its greatest significant when this nation was just getting started and settlers were breaking ground in new territories. Land grants were fairly common. Today, this clause is rather obsolete.

Did you know that because the Supreme Court had such limited authority, for the first ten years of this nation, it convened for only two weeks a year? That was all the time it needed to conduct its business. And there was no Supreme Court house; the justices held court in any spare room at the capitol building.

After the first ten years, they decided it was necessary to convene for at least six to eight weeks but no more than that. It was not until after Roosevelt and the New Deal era, in 1957, that the Supreme Court decided it needed to be a full-time, professional judicial body and convened for nine months a year.

Knowing what limited authority the Supreme Court and the inferior courts have, how do you think it went about justifying a nine-month session? The same way Congress did. They embraced Marxism and started claiming authority it didn't have.

I'm going to present to you some historical court cases and briefly explain the unconstitutionality and thus the criminal activity of the federal courts.

In 1947, in *Everson v. Board of Education*, a christophobe complained about public transportation being used for religious schools. The Supreme Court stated, "The First Amendment has erected a wall between church and state. That wall must be kept high and impregnable. We could not approve the slightest breach."

In 1962, in *Engel v. Vitale*, the Supreme Court eliminated state-sponsored pray stating,

> For this reason, petitioners argue, that State's use of the Regents' prayer in its public school system breaches the constitutional wall of separation between Church and State. We agree with that contention, since we think that the constitutional prohibition against laws respecting an establishment of religion must at least mean that, in this country, it is no part of the business of government to compose official prayers for any group of the American people to recite as a part of a religious program carried on by government.

In *Murray v. Curlett* (1963), the Supreme Court ruled to abolish school prayer and Bible reading. It stated, "Religious freedom, it has long been recognized that government must be neutral and, while protecting all, must prefer none and disparage none."

In 2005, the US Court of Appeals Sixth Circuit ruled in *ACLU v. Mercer County* (Kentucky) that the Ten Commandments could be displayed as part of a larger display of American legal tradition in its courthouse.

In 2005, federal judge John E. Jones III ruled that the Dover school board had violated the Constitution when it established a policy on teaching intelligent design.

> In making this determination we have addressed the seminal question of whether ID (intelligent design) is science. We have concluded that it is not, and moreover that ID cannot uncouple itself from its creationist, and thus religious, antecedents.

I've chosen these case specifically because they all show how this Marxist system of government has targeted and persecuted Christianity. This is a study or another video in and of itself. I will be readdressing these cases and expounding on them in later articles. If you have studied American history and read any of the writings of the founding fathers and their intent of Christianity's role in our culture, you'll know that these opinions are all blatant lies.

Did you notice that each of these cases involved either citizens of the same state or citizen versus a local government? In Article 3, Section 2, which we just looked at, did you see anywhere were it gave the federal courts the authority to try or hear court cases or appeals involving citizens of the same state or citizens versus their local governments? No, it's not there. Just their hearing these cases is a criminal act. These are clear violations of the Eleventh Amendment as well as Article 3. Worse still is the fact that each of these cases is now considered the law of the land—case law.

Remember what Article 1, Section 1 states: "All legislative Powers herein granted shall be vested in a Congress of the United States, which shall consist of a Senate and House of Representatives." Nowhere here do we see that the judicial branch has been given authority to make case law. Instead, it denies it. Case law is illegal in this country. Each time a federal judge legislates from the bench, he is committing a felony. Here is further proof.

The Declaration of Independence listed about twenty-seven reasons we were going to war with Britain. Here are four of them concerning the abuse of British courts.

IN CONGRESS, July 4, 1776.

The unanimous Declaration of the thirteen united States of America,

The history of the present King of Great Britain is a history of repeated injuries and usurpations, all having in direct object the establishment of an absolute Tyranny over these States. To prove this, let Facts be submitted to a candid world …

He has obstructed the Administration of Justice, by refusing his Assent to Laws for establishing Judiciary powers. He has made Judges dependent on his Will alone, for the tenure of their offices, and the amount and payment of their salaries. – meaning they could not be held accountable for their actions. -

He has combined with others to subject us to a jurisdiction foreign to our constitution, and unacknowledged by our laws; giving his Assent to their Acts of pretended Legislation: - meaning British judges were ruling cases outside their jurisdiction, and making case law.

For suspending our own Legislatures, and declaring themselves invested with power to legislate for us in all cases whatsoever. –meaning making case law suspending laws made by local governments on every public issue.

Judicial activism was a problem then; the British courts made case law to restrict its subjects. Do you honestly believe that our founding fathers would set in place a constitution that would allow the same type of abuses? Absolutely not. Case law is an unconstitutional and thus a criminal act in this country.

Do you recall what I taught in my second video, "What Our Founders Gave Us" concerning *Marbury v. Madison*? Marshall examined the Judiciary Act of 1789 subsection 13: "The Supreme Court shall also have appellate jurisdiction from the circuit courts and courts of the several states, in the cases herein after provided for and writs of mandamus." This act of Congress enlarged the Supreme Court's power to include writs of mandamus, and Marshall pointed out that Congress had no authority to violate the Constitution in this manner. The same logic also applies to this same act where it gives the Supreme Court appellate jurisdiction over the state courts. No act or law by Congress can enlarge or decrease the powers of the courts or of itself; only an amendment to the Constitution can do that.

Are these the only crimes our Supreme Court has committed? Let's again look at Obamacare. The Supreme Court ruled that the federal government could mandate citizens to purchase health insurance or be fined or imprisoned. The court claimed it was a tax. There is no way forcing people to purchase protection can be classified as a tax. It goes beyond ridiculous. In my twenty-three years of law enforcement, we called it extortion. Literally what the Supreme Court gave its blessing to is nothing less than extortion. So not only is the Supreme Court guilty of violating the Constitution, it is also guilty of conspiracy and extortion. Why have our presidents and Congress allowed the courts to get away with this? Look at the history of the Marxist Nazi Germany of Hitler. Hitler constantly used his courts to litigate legislation.

The sedition that our past presidents and US legislatures have done can best be called covert insurrection, and yes, it is treasonous, but what our courts are doing is nothing less than open rebellion. There is not one federal judge serving today who shouldn't be impeached. As a matter of fact, they must be impeached for their behavior. The Constitution mandates it. But you know that this Marxist Congress will never do it. They need the courts this way to help them with their full-time professional positions.

If President Donald Trump is serious about draining the swamp, he needs to start with his federal judges. All of them. There is no doubt in my mind that with a good lawyer, he could try every one of them for insurrection and have a state supreme court hear their cases.

Until next time, may the blessings of the Lord be with you. I bless you in the name of the Lord.

CHAPTER FOUR

ARTICLES 6-9

Article 6: Shortcomings Part 1: The Presidency

We don't have a king in this country; most Americans would be quick to tell you that they didn't want one, that they are appalled at the thought of having a monarch or dictator. But do our actions and beliefs coincide with our words? Just watching my countrymen and listening to their beliefs and expectations of our presidents, I am convinced that people are by nature prone to desire a king.

Regardless of how enlightened a person claims to be, subconsciously, all people want to have one person they can turn to to solve all their problems or point a finger when things go wrong. (Aren't we good at pointing fingers in this country?) The simple proof of this is in the manner in which we esteem most of our presidents. After the election on November 4, 2014, when the Republican Party won the majority in Congress, this excerpt was found in the *Western Journal* webpage on November 6. Obama's staff told ABC News,

> You can expect the President to set an aggressive and
> defiant tone tomorrow. You're not going to see any
> mea culpas, no big firings, no change in direction …
> The President is prepared to aggressively pursue
> his agenda using his power of executive authority,
> where he can't work with Congress, and the big one
> is going to be on immigration reform.

The president is going to aggressively pursue his agenda using his power of executive authority where he can't work with Congress.

Let me start this article off with what is not the authority, prerogative, or responsibility of the president. The president has no authority or responsibility to make or propose national policies for the United States except international treaties. The president has no authority to dictate what course of action Congress is to take on any subject. The president has no authority to pick and choose which laws passed by Congress (as long as they are legal) he will enforce. The president has no power or authority to make any law. The president is not on equal footing with Congress; he is subordinate to it. The Constitution does not create three equal branches of federal government; it established a hierarchy with Congress at the top of the food chain and the president below it. (The Supreme Court or judicial branch is at the bottom of the food chain.) So the comment released by Obama's staff displayed total contempt for Congress, the Constitution, and US citizens.

So if the president doesn't have any of these powers, what can he do? To answer that we need to look at Article 1, Section 7 and Article 2, Sections 1–3 of the Constitution. These sections enumerate and define the authority of the president and also set limitations on the president. Yes, the president has limits, and rather tight limits to be precise.

In Article 1, Section 7, the president is given the power of veto. If the president finds a bill in violation of the Constitution in any way, he is to veto that bill.

Every Bill ... shall, before it become a Law, be presented to the President of the United States: If he approve he shall sign it, but if not he shall return it, with his Objections to that House in which it shall have originated ...

Every Order, Resolution, or Vote to which the Concurrence of the Senate and House of Representatives may be necessary (except on a question of Adjournment) shall be presented to the President of the United States; and before the Same shall take Effect, shall be approved by him, or being disapproved by him. — Article 1, Section 7

This is the first of the checks and balances in place that is supposed to prevent abuse of power by the various branches of the federal government. There are a total of six in place (the seventh was eliminated by the Seventeenth Amendment), some for each branch to hold in check the other branches. Even so, it was the intent of the writers of the Constitution that for the most part, each branch of the federal government would work independently of the other two. This is easily confirmed by reading Federalist Paper 47.

Let's look at Article 2, which specifically spells out the powers and limitations of the president.

The executive Power shall be vested in a President of the United States of America. — Article 2, Section 1

Notice that the executive powers or the powers to run the federal government are exclusive to the president. Nowhere in the Constitution is any executive power granted to Congress; thus Congress has no authority to have oversight over any department of the federal government. Congress's only job is to make laws. It is illegal for it to try to run the government as that would be in violation of this clause. Nor does Congress have the power to enlarge or decrease the executive power; it has no power to make laws limiting the powers of the executive authority that would impede the effectiveness of the president. Such laws would be in violation of this clause and therefor unconstitutional and void. The same holds true for the judicial branch.

Sections 2 and 3 spell out what those powers consist of and what they are limited to. Let us read Sections 2 and 3. This won't take long; neither section is lengthy.

> The President shall be Commander in Chief of the Army and Navy of the United States, and of the Militia of the several States, when called into the actual Service of the United States; he may require the Opinion, in writing, of the principal Officer in each of the executive Departments, upon any Subject relating to the Duties of their respective Offices, and he shall have Power to grant Reprieves and Pardons for Offences against the United States, except in Cases of Impeachment.

> He shall have Power, by and with the Advice and Consent of the Senate, to make Treaties, provided two thirds of the Senators present concur; and he shall nominate, and by and with the Advice and Consent of the Senate, shall appoint Ambassadors, other public Ministers and Consuls, Judges of the supreme Court, and all other Officers of the United States, whose Appointments are not herein otherwise provided for, and which shall be established by Law: but the Congress may by Law vest the Appointment of such inferior Officers, as they think proper, in the President alone, in the Courts of Law, or in the Heads of Departments.

The President shall have Power to fill up all Vacancies that may happen during the Recess of the Senate, by granting Commissions which shall expire at the End of their next Session. —Section 2

He shall from time to time give to the Congress Information of the State of the Union, and recommend to their Consideration such Measures as he shall judge necessary and expedient; he may, on extraordinary Occasions, convene both Houses, or either of them, and in Case of Disagreement between them, with Respect to the Time of Adjournment, he may adjourn them to such Time as he shall think proper; he shall receive Ambassadors and other public Ministers; he shall take Care that the Laws be faithfully executed, and shall Commission all the Officers of the United States. —Section 3

Both sections take up barely half a page. This is because the president was not given a whole lot of power though the power he is given is very significant. This was done intentionally by our founding fathers for two clear reasons. The intent of this Constitution and the founders was to secure the freedom of America's citizens. Their goal was to ensure our liberty. We had just fought the Revolutionary War to become independent of tyranny under King George III. The men who wrote the Constitution despised this form of rule and so designed our central government so that we would never have a despot. To do so, they greatly limited or restricted what the president could do, and they made Congress, which represents the people and the states, a custodian over the president. So this chain of command is of course the second reason the Constitution was written limiting the president. Let's break down Sections 2–3 of Article 2 to see exactly what our founders decided to give the president in the form of power, and let's examine Congress's control over him.

As we see in the first paragraph of Section 2, the first duty of the president in clause 1 is that of commander in chief of the army and navy. The president is not given the power to declare war (this power is given to Congress in Article 1, Section 8, Paragraph 11), but when we are at war, the president is the highest ranking officer in the land, and while in a war where there is a clear and present danger, the president can call the states' militias into the service of the federal government as well. This is of course the most important power of the president, and it has to be used with extreme prudence.

After the attack on the World Trade Center on September 11, 2001, President Bush pronounced that we were in a war with the goal of eliminating international terrorism—the war on terror. The problem with this was that one, it was too ambiguous. The standard for going to war is a clear and present danger. Terrorists strike randomly and then disperse for long periods, so terrorism is never really clear and present. Many might argue with this and state I'm nitpicking, but as long as people don't get along, there will always be groups that stand up for a misbegotten cause, so this war on terror will never end. This means that the militia will be perpetually at the command of the president. This is not a good thing as it will and has led to abuse of presidential power.

The second problem is that it is an international war. Clear and present means clear and present threat to America, not every other nation as well. Our founders did not set up the power of commander in chief so we could become the world's police. Whom do you think foots the bill? This is just too tremendous a burden on the American taxpayer—you and me.

Clause 2 of Paragraph 1 states, "He may require the Opinion, in writing, of the principal Officer in each of the executive Departments, upon any Subject relating to the Duties of their respective Offices."

Have you ever wondered what the term *executive order* meant? This clause gives the president the power of issuing executive orders. Take a close look at this clause. Do you notice how limited in scope this power is? The president can issue orders directed only at the executive branch, nowhere else.

Executive orders were never intended to be laws but directives to an officer of one of the departments of the executive branch. The president has no power whatsoever to make laws; Article 1, Section 1 of the Constitution states, "All legislative Powers herein granted shall be vested in a Congress of the United States, which shall consist of a Senate and House of Representatives." The word *all* at the beginning of the first paragraph of the first Article of the Constitution did not appear by chance; it was a deliberate act to let the American people and future generations know that only Congress had the power to make laws in the federal government, not the president or the judiciary. The founders wanted this to be a free nation and to ensure our freedom from tyrants. If they had given the president or the courts the ability to make laws, that would have undermined their goal and the president and the Supreme Court would be nothing more than despots. This is why neither the president nor the federal courts have the power to make laws. At least legally they can't make laws. Neither the president nor the courts represent the people. Their jobs are entirely different. The president runs the federal government, not America, and enforces legal laws passed by Congress, and the courts uphold the laws legally passed by Congress. That's it.

For a president to make an executive order and declare it a law of the land would be a violation of Article 1, Section 1 of the Constitution and a criminal act. He'd have to be impeached. Remember how I stated in my first article that FDR was the greatest traitor this country has ever known? Well, he is the biggest thief this nation has ever known as well. In 1933, he issued Executive Order 6102 mandating that all people turn over their gold to the federal government. His stated reason was that Americans were hoarding their gold and it was slowing the progress of recovery from the Great Depression. First, neither the federal government nor any government has any authority or say over what we the people do with our private property; that is a protection by the Fourth Amendment.

Roosevelt also violated Article 1, Section 1: "All legislative

Powers herein granted shall be vested in a Congress of the United States, which shall consist of a Senate and House of Representatives." He violated Article 4, Section 4, and this clause of Article 2, Section 2. This executive order was an act of a dictator. So was every other executive order issued since then that a president has declared as law outside the confines of the federal government. And this act by itself shows which form of Marxist republic Roosevelt set in place. Oh, the federal government is still hoarding that gold, which is truly the inheritance of all the descendants of those who were gullible enough to turn over their private gold reserves.

Let's continue to examine the limitations of the president. Take a look at the third and last clause of Section 2, Paragraph 1: "He shall have Power to grant Reprieves and Pardons for Offences against the United States, except in Cases of Impeachment." The Constitution gives the president the power to pardon a person who has committed a federal offense, someone who has broken a legal federal law. This is what is meant by offenses against the United States. This clause does not give the president the power to pardon someone who has committed a crime against a state or has broken a state law. Only the governor of a state has the power to pardon a citizen of the state for state offenses, and that only if the state constitution grants that power to the governor.

Let's move on to the second paragraph of Section 2, Article 2. There are again only three clauses in this paragraph, and three more powers granted. The first clause reads, "He shall have Power, by and with the Advice and Consent of the Senate, to make Treaties, provided two thirds of the Senators present concur."

The second most important job of the president is to be the ambassador to foreign nations for the United States. With this responsibility, he is given the power to make treaties. The only way the president can influence the economic standing of the United States is through his treaties. The last presidents over the last thirty years have failed miserably in this regard. So far, only President Trump has made any foreign policies that benefit the people of this nation. Yet this power to make treaties is severely limited. He can make only treaties covering issues that Congress has given him permission to make, and once he drafts a treaty, he must get the approval of Congress before he can implement it.

In addition to this, Article 6, Paragraph 3 states, "All Treaties made, or which shall be made, under the Authority of the United States." The authority of the United States is the Constitution. What Article 6 is saying is that all treaties must be in conformity with the Constitution and that neither the president nor Congress can allow any treaty to pass that violates even one clause of the Constitution. Even though the president is given the great responsibility of representing this country before other nations, that responsibility is severely limited and controlled by Congress. The president answers to them, not the other way around.

Let's look at the second clause of Paragraph 2, Section 2.

> He shall nominate, and by and with the Advice and Consent of the Senate, shall appoint Ambassadors, other public Ministers and Consuls, Judges of the supreme Court, and all other Officers of the United States, whose Appointments are not herein otherwise provided for, and which shall be established by Law.

This second clause is the power of appointment. For the most part, the president is given the authority to determine who he is going to have to work for him. But notice again that this power is still controlled by whom? Congress! The president can nominate ambassadors and public minsters to help him complete his job as the ambassador of the United States, he can nominate new judges when a position opens up, and he can nominate the people he wants as heads of the executive departments to help him run the federal government. This is good because to be effective, the president has to be able to work well with the people under him. If he picks the wrong people, it falls on him. Still, all nominees must be approved by Congress.

The third and final clause of Paragraph 2 doesn't really give the president any additional powers; it is still concerned with the power of appointment, but it does give Congress the authority to give the president greater authority in respect to appointing persons to inferior offices, the people who work for the people who report to the president. It states, "Congress may by Law vest the Appointment of such inferior Officers, as they think proper, in the President alone, in the Courts of Law, or in the Heads of Departments." Again, you see the power of the president is controlled by Congress, not the other way around. Congress can give this power and can take that power away. This is the only clause in the entire Constitution that allows Congress the power to enlarge or decrease the power of a branch of government—for the president— and only in this matter. Otherwise, only an amendment to the Constitution can enlarge or decrease the powers of any of the branches of the federal government.

The third and last paragraph of Section 2 of Article 2 contains only one clause and only one power. That power is to grant a temporary commission to someone as an acting department head if and only if something happened to an existing department head when Congress is in recess; this includes incapacitation due to hospitalization, death, or severe personal matters. In such a case, the president can replace that department head for one session of Congress and then find a permanent replacement that Congress approves of. The paragraph reads, "The President shall have Power to fill up all Vacancies that may happen during the Recess of the Senate, by granting Commissions which shall expire at the End of their next Session."

So you can see that all six powers granted to the president in Section 2 of Article 2 are tightly controlled by Congress, clearly the dominant branch of government here with the president in a subordinate role.

Section 3 of Article 2 has five clauses; the first states, "He shall from time to time give to the Congress Information of the State of the Union, and recommend to their Consideration such Measures as he shall judge necessary and expedient." We need to take a close look at this clause as this receives the most abuse from the executive branch. This clause has been violated by the last several presidents of whom President Barack Obama was the greatest offender. President Trump is following suit, but as he is a businessman turned politician and not a polished politician as prior presidents were, I'm inclined to grant him some grace until he learns the true duties of the president. This clause of the Constitution is called the State of the Union Address. Read this clause again and keep in mind that the founders knew the literal meaning of words and meant this to be taken as written.

At least once a year the President is to make an assessment as to how well the federal government is doing and how well the nation, in general, is doing. Then, after making his assessment he is to address Congress giving them his evaluation. After giving the congress his evaluation he is able to make recommendations that he believes would resolve any problems he observed. Notice that it states that he is only given the authority to make recommendations. This clause is not giving the President power to make, demand, push for, or command a policy or law to be made by Congress. The President can only make a onetime suggestion as to what he thinks should be done, and Congress only needs to considerate it, and not act on it if they do not deem the suggestion is in the best interest of the people or if the suggestion is in violation of the Constitution. This is all that this clause allows the President to do. Anything beyond this is a violation of the Constitution. Anything beyond this usurps the power of Congress, the power to make laws. Remember it is the Congress that is our representatives and the laws that it enacts should reflect the desires of the people not the demands of the President. When a President violates this clause by making demands of the Congress, he is taking on the role of a despot. Our Founders designed this Constitution to prevent Despotism. This is why this clause limits the President in only giving his recommendation and nothing more. This is a clause all Americans should know well and never allow it to be violated.

The second clause of Section 3 states,

> He may, on extraordinary Occasions, convene both Houses, or either of them, and in Case of Disagreement between them, with Respect to the Time of Adjournment, he may adjourn them to such Time as he shall think proper.

This clause is contingent on an extraordinary occasion—war. America is on the verge of being attacked. Our founders never intended Congress to be a full-time job; it is required to meet only one time a year. The founders expected the elected officials to meet, take care of business, and go home. Because they had limited the authority of the federal government to so few things, they understood that all the laws needed to run the federal government would soon be made and that only minor adjustments would be needed after that or when new authority was granted the United States government by new amendments. They realized that Congress might not be in session when this nation was attacked. As stated earlier, only Congress has the power to declare war.

This clause gives the president the power to call all members of Congress together in a time of emergency so they could legally declare war and so he could go about the business of protecting this nation. The purpose of any government is to protect its people, not control their lives. Well, except for socialist/Marxist governments. Marxism is about total enslavement of its people. Anyway, this clause gives the president the power to convene Congress in an emergency and the power to tell its members to go home after they've resolved the emergency if they can't figure it's time for them to go home on their own. Again, this is an extremely rare power of the president and again very limited.

The second paragraph of Section 2 implies that the president is the ambassador for the United States by granting him the power to appoint ambassadors and ministers and the power to draft treaties, but the third clause of Section 3 states specifically that this is one of his primary duties: "He shall receive Ambassadors and other public Ministers."

I am going to jump to the fifth clause of Section 3 before addressing the fourth because I need to spend more time on the fourth. The fifth clause states, "… and shall Commission all the Officers of the United States." All officers in the navy and army receive their commissions from the president. That simple.

Now let's take a close look at the fourth clause of Section 3 of Article 2: "He shall take Care that the Laws be faithfully executed." This short and direct clause is very significant. Do you see the word *shall*? It signifies that this is not an option. He has no choice but to uphold and enforce all legal laws made under the Constitution. It is not within his authority to pick and choose which laws passed by Congress he intends to enforce, and immigration laws fall under the authority of Congress (Article 1, Section 8, Paragraph 4). Look at what President Obama did with the illegal immigrants in this nation as stated in the article in the *Western Journal* I mentioned earlier.

The President is prepared to aggressively pursue his agenda using his power of executive authority, where he can't work with Congress, and the big one is going to be on immigration reform.

We see that he violated this clause of the Constitution. The president has the power to grant pardons, but this power is designed for specific cases where there are exigent circumstances with a particular offender. It was never meant as a way for the president to circumvent the law, but this is exactly what this president did. By giving a blanket pardon or amnesty to millions of criminal, illegal immigrants, and yes, the president can pardon only criminals, it is an act in defiance of the law. The president is conducting a criminal act. Violating the Constitution is a crime, and Section 4 of Article 2 explains what should/must happen to a president who does not properly execute the laws of the land.

The President, Vice President and all civil Officers of the United States, shall be removed from Office on Impeachment for, and Conviction of, Treason, Bribery, or other high Crimes and Misdemeanors.

I stated earlier that the Constitution is the law of the land as mandated by Article 6, Paragraph 2 of the Constitution and is predominant over all other laws in this nation; the Constitution carries the same weight as the severest law made under its authority. If a president is to be impeached for a felony (High Crimes), he and any other civil officer of the United States are to be impeached for deliberate violations of the Constitution as well.

I want to look at the oath of office in the last paragraph in Section 1 of Article 2.

Before he enter on the Execution of his Office, he shall take the following Oath or Affirmation: "I do solemnly swear (or affirm) that I will faithfully execute the Office of President of the United States, and will to the best of my Ability, preserve, protect and defend the Constitution of the United States."

This oath and the oaths required in Article 6,

The Senators and Representatives before mentioned, and the Members of the several State Legislatures, and all executive and judicial Officers, both of the United States and of the several States, shall be bound by Oath or Affirmation, to support this Constitution.

is the fifth and most powerful of the checks and balances in the Constitution. Do you remember in my prior article how I asked how someone could support the Constitution and enforce an unconstitutional law at the same time? You can't. The power of the oath of office gives the president the power to declare any law, act of Congress, executive order made by prior presidents or his own executive orders, or any court decision that is repugnant of the Constitution void. His oath prohibits him from enforcing an unconstitutional act, so he is forced to declare it void. The same is true for the governors, judges, and members of Congress of each state. The oath they are required to take to support the Constitution prohibits them from enforcing an unconstitutional law, executive order, or court decision. They have to declare them void or end up in violation of this clause and commit a criminal act. Remember that the Constitution is the law of the land binding on all government. It's a crime for them to violate it.

Neither the president nor state government officials have to have the unconstitutional law repealed by Congress or wait for the verdict of the Supreme Court; they have this power all by themselves. This is the power of the oath. Actually, the Supreme Court has already acknowledged this power by its ruling opinion in *Marbury v. Madison*. This required oath is the only place in the Constitution that hints of the power of judicial review for a federal judge. Otherwise, Marshall's ruling would have violated his own opinion. Article 3 doesn't give the Supreme Court the power of judicial review.

So the power of the oath gives the Supreme Court the power to declare an act of Congress unconstitutional; it also gives the state government and the president that same power. It has to be so. Otherwise, explain how a person could take an oath to support the Constitution and enforce an unconstitutional law at the same time.

President Trump has voided some of Obama's executive orders through countering executive orders and is debating if he should void more. The propagandists or press debate if he can. The answer is he must. To fulfil his oath, President Trump has to void every unconstitutional law, agency, edict, and ruling made by Congress and the federal courts. If he wants to truly drain the swamp, he has all the power he needs to do it. All he has to say is, "Obamacare is in violation of the Tenth Amendment" and is void. That's all it takes.

As we looked at the authority of and the limitations put on the president, it becomes obvious that he was never given the power to make laws for the United States or to dictate anything to Congress. The opposite is true. In many instances, Congress dictates what the president can do.

The president was never meant to be the ruler of this nation, and he has no power whatsoever to act in this capacity. The purpose of the president is merely to maintain the operations of the executive branch of the federal government, nothing more. Our presidents have gained the power of all-powerful despots through the uneducation of the people and no way else. It is because of our national ignorance that he wields the power he does. The president is in no way as important as we make him out to be, and he is easily replaced. The Constitution is written so that he can be easily replaced. This is obvious by the following clauses of the Constitution: the original writing of Article 2, Section 1, Paragraph 6, and Amendment 20, Section 3, and Amendment 25, Sections 1, 3, and 4.

The most dangerous thing the people of the United States can do is allow our presidents to act beyond the capacity granted them by the Constitution, which was meant to ensure our freedom so we would never know despotism. But we the people must act to keep our freedom and quit gradually giving up our rights. National slavery is always just around the corner when you give a president too much rein. —March 17, 2015

Article 7: Shortcomings Part 2: Congress

What political branch is guaranteed to subject a free people to slavery? By its very nature, it has to. It's a full-time professional legislature whether it be the federal or state or local lawmakers.

Take this analogy. If you were to throw a frog into a pot of boiling water, the frog would jump out of course as it acts to save itself. But if you put it into a pot of cool water, the frog would stay put because it would feel safe. If you gradually increase the temperature of the water, the frog would acclimate to that. Increase the temperature a bit more, and as it acclimates, it would still feel safe. You keep on doing this until you finally boil the fog alive; all the while, the frog feels safe.

This is the same with a free people and full-time professional legislators. By their very nature, the legislators have to make laws to justify their existence. With each new law they enact, they strip away a little more of our rights and freedom. And the people acclimate. In time, the free people become slaves of the state while all the while feeling safe.

In my article 5, "The Rights of the States Part 2 and in article 6 Shortcommings Part 1," I discussed the two weaker branches of the federal government, the executive and the judicial branches. Now it is time to look at the most powerful branch of the federal government, the legislative. Sounds pretty impressive, doesn't it—the most powerful branch of the federal government? Yet as impressive as this sounds, our founders really limited the power it gave Congress; reason being they wanted to keep this a free nation and ensure our liberty.

Whom is it easier for you to keep tabs on, your state government officials or your members of Congress in DC? Whom can you more readily see with a problem, your state representatives or your representatives in DC? What are you more aware of, what is going on in your own backyard or what is going on in DC?

The Constitution declares we the people as the true authority of this nation, not the delegates we elect. We call them delegates because we have delegated our authority to them. When we delegate, we aren't giving up our authority; on the contrary, we are extending that authority to someone else. We still retain our authority and have the power to take back or retract that authority. It is much easier for us to control our local governments than a government further removed from us. So the way we control a government removed from us is to limit the power we give it. The larger the government, the lesser the power we grant it. This is exactly what our founders did; they delegated those powers to the central (federal) government that would benefit the nation as a whole while reserving the greater powers for the states, which are more readily in our control. (Read Federalist Papers 40–50 especially 45.)

Article 1 of the Constitution defines the powers or authority granted to Congress. Did you notice that the legislative branch was first on the founders' list of concerns and not the presidency? The power to make laws is the true power of any government. Look at the very first paragraph of the first section of the first article of our Constitution: "All legislative Powers herein granted shall be vested in a Congress of the United States, which shall consist of a Senate and House of Representatives." All legislative power, the power to make laws, is exclusively granted to Congress. No such power is reserved for or granted to the president or the judiciary. This means that it is a violation of this section of the Constitution if they try to make laws. It's a criminal act. As I stated earlier, this was meant to prevent either of the two lesser branches of the federal government from having too much power and becoming despots rather than servants of the people.

I am not going to get into the process of making laws as spelled out in the Constitution; instead, I will concentrate on the type of authority or subject matter our founders gave Congress to wield or make laws on.

The only other power granted to Congress is the power to impeach. In Section 2, the House of Representatives is given the sole power of impeachment. In Section 3, the Senate is given the sole power to try all impeachments. It also states,

> Judgment in Cases of Impeachment shall not extend further than to removal from Office, and disqualification to hold and enjoy any Office of honor, Trust, or Profit, under the United States: but the Party convicted **shall** nevertheless be liable and subject to Indictment, Trial, Judgment and Punishment, according to Law.

So for what reasons can an elected official be impeached? We find that answer in Article 2, Section 4 of the Constitution.

> The President, Vice President and all civil Officers of the United States, **shall** be removed from Office on Impeachment for, and Conviction of, Treason, Bribery, or other high Crimes (meaning felonies) and Misdemeanors.

A president can't be impeached just because a representative doesn't like his policies or him. If a representative filed for an impeachment for these reasons, he would be in violation of this article and himself be subject to impeachment. This is the only other job granted Congress, and it is performed on only the rarest occasions. With our current government, it should be commonplace.

In Section 5, Paragraph 2 of Article 1, Congress is given the power to be self-regulating.

> Each House may determine the Rules of its Proceedings, punish its Members for disorderly Behaviour, and, with the Concurrence of two thirds, expel a Member.

As far as oversight is concerned, this is the extent of their power, and they don't have the authority to add any powers via an act of Congress. Only an amendment to the Constitution can grant them more power.

Article 2, Section 1 states, "The executive Power shall be vested in a President of the United States of America." Do you notice it doesn't say anything about Congress having the power to run the government? When we see these congressional oversight committees or congressional hearings requiring a department head to justify his actions, they are in violation of Article 1, Section 5, and Article 2, Section 1. Exerting the power of oversight over the president or federal agencies is a criminal act on their part, meaning that under Article 2, Section 4, they have to be impeached.

Section 7 states, "All Bills for raising Revenue shall originate in the House of Representatives." This means that appropriation bills must be made by the House of Representatives, which is under the control of the people. If Congress is spending too much money, it's ultimately our fault for putting the same representatives back in office.

It does say in Article 1 Section 6,

> They shall in all Cases, **except** Treason, Felony and Breach of the Peace, be privileged from Arrest during their Attendance at the Session of their respective Houses, and in going to and returning from the same.

If they can be arrested for treason, felonies, and misdemeanors under this section, what then are they privileged from arrest from? Only petty offenses; they can't be given parking tickets, speeding tickets, and other petty traffic tickets and such. They are subject to the full extent of the law for all other crimes just as the rest of us are though they will argue tooth and nail that they are above all law. Our founders expected us and rightly so to hold our elected officials to the highest standards, not the lowest standards we see today. But truly who is to blame but us?

Now we come to the meat and potatoes of congressional power. Section 8 of Article 1 lists the majority of the powers Congress can make laws on and where I plan to go into some detail explaining. Let's read Section 8 and then break it down.

> The Congress shall have Power To lay and collect Taxes, Duties, Imposts and Excises, to pay the Debts and provide for the common Defence and general Welfare of the United States; but all Duties, Imposts and Excises shall be uniform throughout the United States;

To borrow Money on the credit of the United States;

To regulate Commerce with foreign Nations, and among the several States, and with the Indian Tribes;

To establish an uniform Rule of Naturalization, and uniform Laws on the subject of Bankruptcies throughout the United States;

To coin Money, regulate the Value thereof, and of foreign Coin, and fix the Standard of Weights and Measures;

To provide for the Punishment of counterfeiting the Securities and current Coin of the United States;

To establish Post Offices and post Roads;

To promote the Progress of Science and useful Arts, by securing for limited Times to Authors and Inventors the exclusive Right to their respective Writings and Discoveries;

To constitute Tribunals inferior to the supreme Court;

To define and punish Piracies and Felonies committed on the high Seas, and Offences against the Law of Nations;

To declare War, grant Letters of Marque and Reprisal, and make Rules concerning Captures on Land and Water;

To raise and support Armies, but no Appropriation of Money to that Use shall be for a longer Term than two Years;

To provide and maintain a Navy;

To make Rules for the Government and Regulation of the land and naval Forces;

To provide for calling forth the Militia to execute the Laws of the Union, suppress Insurrections and repel Invasions;

To provide for organizing, arming, and disciplining, the Militia, and for governing such Part of them as may be employed in the Service of the United States, reserving to the States respectively, the Appointment of the Officers, and the Authority of training the Militia according to the discipline prescribed by Congress;

To exercise exclusive Legislation in all Cases whatsoever, over such District (not exceeding ten Miles square) as may, by Cession of particular States, and the Acceptance of Congress, become the Seat of the Government of the United States, and to exercise like Authority over all Places purchased by the Consent of the Legislature of the State in which the Same shall be, for the Erection of Forts, Magazines, Arsenals, dock-Yards, and other needful Buildings;--And

To make all Laws which shall be necessary and proper for carrying into Execution the foregoing Powers, and all other Powers vested by this

Constitution in the Government of the United
States, or in any Department or Officer thereof.

I want to spend most of our time examining this section of
Article 1 so we can concentrate on the true authority of our federal
government and show how it is abusing that authority and usurping
the states' authority. But before that, I want to quickly cover the
other subject matter granted by the Constitution that Congress has
the power to make laws on. The additional legislative powers come
from various amendments, and for the most part, the amendments
are all the law necessary to achieve the goal of the legislators, and
most of them are well ingrained in the American psyche and readily
followed. But a few such as the Third Amendment give Congress
very limited leeway for additional laws.

The Third Amendment gives Congress the power to make laws
in regard to quartering US troops in private homes in time of war.
However, in modern times, when hotels are in abundance, this
power is really obsolete. But should the need ever arise, Congress
has that power.

In all the rest of these amendments is verbiage that states that
Congress can enforce the new article (or amendment) by appropriate
legislation; laws in conformity with the Constitution. Congress can
make no law to support a new amendment that violates any other
section of the Constitution. Congress has no power whatsoever
to make a law that would supersede the Constitution. This was
confirmed in the 1803 case *Marbury v. Madison*, the same case by
which the Supreme Court acknowledged its authority to declare a
law unconstitutional.

In 1803, the Supreme Court established its power
to declare an act of Congress unconstitutional.
The case, Marbury v. Madison, involved an act of
Congress which enlarged the original jurisdiction
of the Supreme Court. The Court said that a law

which is repugnant to the Constitution is void
and that congress lacked the power to enlarge or
decrease the Supreme Court's original jurisdiction.
—Federal Law Enforcement Training Center Legal
Text 1/96

The following amendments increase the scope of authority that
Congress can make laws on but only marginally. Amendment 13
allows Congress to make laws that abolish involuntary servitude
and slavery except when a person is duly convicted of a crime.
Amendment 14 in Section 3 gives Congress the power to pass laws
granting a person denied the privilege of serving in an elected office
due to insurrection the ability to serve in that capacity. Amendment
15 allows Congress the power to make laws allowing all citizens
regardless of race and color the right to vote. Amendment 16 allows
income tax laws. Amendment 18 was repealed. Amendment 19
allows laws for women to vote. Amendment 23 allows for laws for
the District of Columbia to vote. Amendment 24 allows for laws
prohibiting poll taxes. And finally, Amendment 26 allows laws that
let eighteen-year-olds vote.

That's it! Simple. As I said, most of these amendments addressed
the problems all on their own with no need for additional laws.
Some amendments address administrative powers, but as they are
in-house regulations and don't really affect the populace, I did not
mention them.

Let's get back to the meat and potatoes of the Constitution
and congressional power and examine Article 1, Section 8. As does
all well-composed literature, Section 8 starts off with an opening
sentence stating the subject, which is explained in the following
sentences. Nothing is left to be misconstrued. However, corrupt
politicians rely on the uneducation of the people and come up
with clever but deceitful ways to circumvent the limitations of the
Constitution. Let's take a look how. Here again is the first part or
clause of Section 8.

> The Congress shall have Power To lay and collect
> Taxes, Duties, Imposts and Excises, to pay the
> Debts and provide for the common Defence and
> general Welfare of the United States; but all Duties,
> Imposts and Excises shall be uniform throughout
> the United States.

If we were to name this clause for reference purposes, it would be titled the uniform taxation clause. Actually, there are two clauses in this paragraph, but they are so closely related that one title can be given to both. What these clauses do is exactly what they say they do; they allow the federal government to collect taxes—we all know what they are—duties are taxes on imported and exported goods, imposts—taxes on goods imported and also known as customs—and excises, taxes on merchandise bought. The power granted in these two clauses is to collect taxes. The purpose is to pay off government debts, provide for national defense, and provide for some common national needs. This is what is meant by general welfare. I don't believe I have to go into too much detail as to what debts are. If the government buys something, it is obligated to pay for it. Simple.

The terms *common defense* and *general welfare* are a little more ambiguous; if left by themselves, they could be construed to mean anything Congress wanted them to mean. However, our founders were much more intelligent than that and continued to write the rest of Section 8 to specifically spell out what they meant Congress to have power to make laws on to support the common defense and general welfare. The next seventeen enumerated sentences define the extent of authority of the federal government.

Before I list the powers the federal government has, I need to explain exactly what a clause is and just as important is not. The definition our founders understood is "a subdivision of a sentence, in which the words are inseparably connected with each other in sense and cannot, with propriety, be separated by a point: a distinct stipulation, condition, proviso, grant, covenant." -- *American Dictionary of The English Language*, Noah Webster, 1828.

For example, in the first sentence of this section, we have only two clauses. The first grants the various taxation and states the purposes for those taxes. The second clause states that the taxation must be uniform throughout the United States. The purposes are inseparable from the distinct grants as the purposes (paying debts, national defense, and general welfare) are the reasons for the taxation.

So now we get to take a look at how the federal government and especially Congress misinterprets the Constitution to usurp the power of state governments. What they do is subcategorize the clause. In the case of the first clause, they take the term *general welfare*, actually just the word *welfare*, and make it a stand-alone clause; they claim that the word *welfare* gives them the power to make welfare laws, laws concerning public acts that the states and the citizens of the United States must obey.

Does this make any sense to you? Remember, I already covered Article 4, and it was written after this portion of the Constitution. It states full faith and credit; all authority for public acts is given to state governments. If this is so, our founding fathers made quite a contradiction. The reality is that our founding fathers did not make a mistake, and as stated earlier, the term *general welfare* is just a general term in the opening statement to introduce the actual powers enumerated in the seventeen following supporting sentences. Basic grammar.

Yet through this misconstruction and abuse of power, Congress has been able through the years to illegally establish the Departments of Labor, Education, Housing and Urban Development and many other agencies with their corresponding laws. All of these and many others are the exclusive prerogative of the states. But through masterful manipulation, these powers have been obtained by the federal government, and very few are the wiser.

In addition to these federal agencies, each state has its own corresponding agency, meaning we have redundancy in governmental tasking. This means you and I are paying more taxes than necessary to support these functions. The states have all the ability necessary to accomplish these tasks without the interference of the federal government. There is just no need for the federal government to get involved with these social realms, except they want power.

Let's look at the actual powers granted to the federal government by looking at the supporting sentences that explain what our founding fathers meant by common defense and general welfare. After each of the supporting sentences, I will indicate whether it falls under paying the debts, common defense, or general welfare.

The first supporting sentence reads, "To borrow Money on the credit of the United States" (paying debts). This clause allows Congress to pass appropriation bills even when the federal government is short on cash by borrowing the money. This was intended to be a limited power to be used in dire need, yet our modern Congress has made this a standard operating procedure. This incompetence alone is all the proof I need to support my statement that the states don't need the federal government meddling with their jurisdiction. To have good credit, you are expected to pay back a loan in a timely manner. With our trillions of dollars of national debt and billions of dollars of deficit spending, the US government can be classified only as a bad credit risk. Again, Congress's incompetence makes not only the US look bad but also we the people.

The second supporting sentence is the most abused and misconstrued clause in this entire section of Article 1 and possibly in the entire Constitution: "To regulate Commerce with foreign Nations, and among the several States, and with the Indian Tribes" (general welfare). This is technically only one clause with regulating commerce as the subject; the rest of the clause describes what commerce is being regulated. However, scholars (I use the term tongue in cheek) divide it into the foreign nations commerce clause, the interstate commerce clause, and the Indian tribes commerce clause.

Let us take a look at Webster's dictionary of 1828 to get a

clear understanding of what our founding fathers understood what commerce was and what they were intending this power to entail.

> In a general sense, an interchange or mutual change of goods, wares, productions, or property of any kind, between nations or individuals, either by barter, or by purchase and sale, trade; traffick. Foreign commerce is the trade which one nation carries on with another; inland commerce, or inland trade, is the trade in the exchange of commodities between citizens of the same nation or state.

This definition is quite specific as was the intent of our founding fathers. Their intent was to allow the federal government to regulate the traffic of goods, finished products that were designed for sale, from state to state, from the US to other nations, and with the Indian tribes. It gives them only the power to regulate finished products being transported for sale. Basically, they can regulate what is being trafficked and ensure that the labeling on the goods is honest. That's the extent of the power granted by this clause. Yet our Congress has made laws that far exceed the power granted to it by the Constitution. How has it gotten away with making such illegal laws?

I mentioned in earlier articles that I used some video of Robert Natelson, a professor of constitutional law, who gave a presentation to a group of Tea Party members in Helena, Montana, a few years back, as part of my public presentation on the Constitution. I am going to give you the transcript of one of those video clips as it explains in detail how our federal government came about violating the Constitution and usurping the states' authority.

> The Congress will have power to … and let's skip down to the third clause, To regulate Commerce with foreign Nations, and among the several States,

and with the Indian Tribes. This third clause is called the commerce clause and you can see it gives Congress three separate powers. Congress has the power to regulate commerce with foreign nations, which is the foreign commerce clause. It has the power to regulate commerce with, ah among the several States, we call that the interstate commerce clause, and it has the power to regulate commerce with the Indian tribes. We call that the Indian commerce clause ... Under the modern formulation that the Supreme Court has, the Congress may regulate commerce, and it may regulate the economic activities substantially effecting commerce. That is the language the Supreme Court used ... umm under the commerce clause, Congress clearly has the power to regulate the transport and the terms of the passage of the clothing from State to State. Under the necessary and proper clause, Congress has the power to insist that the labeling of product going from State to State be honest and not deceptive. That's pretty much as the commerce clause and the necessary and proper clause go at least according to the original understanding. Under the New Deal cases Congress says, well under the necessary and proper clause, we can not only regulate the transport of the clothes and the labeling of the clothes, we can regulate the clothes manufactures too. We can regulate the folks who make the clothes even if they are only within one State. And that is in fact the current law of the Supreme Court. ... This Constitution was written for a relatively small government. It was not written for a government that controls thirty sum odd percent of the American gross domestic product. Okay! So when the people complain of the unresponsiveness of the Congress, or the arrogance of bureaucrats, or the level of the taxes, or whatever, you have to keep in mind this is largely a product of the fact that we have taken a form of government that is designed for a mostly free people and changed it into a government that regulates virtually every aspects of our lives. That was not what the government was set up to do. So you get all kinds of problems.

Do you see how we have been deceived? The biggest problem I had with Natelson when he made these statements was that he made them with such a defeatist attitude. It was as if that was the way it was and there was nothing anybody could do about it. This is so wrong. What he said was right, but there is a lot we the people can do to rectify the problem. First, we have to realize there is a problem, but we have been so uneducated in this country for so long that the vast majority of us think this is the way America is supposed to be run.

I explained that the Supreme Court has no power to make laws let alone make new definitions for words just so it can expand the power of the government. This is precisely what it has done.

Did you notice when Natelson stated these changes came about? It was during the era of Franklin D. Roosevelt's New Deal—socialism wrapped in a pretty bow. Roosevelt tricked the American people into going from being a free people under a constitutional republic to being an enslaved people under socialism. In my first article, I said that all forms of socialism were slave/master relationships in which the people were the slaves to the state and the government was the master. Our ancestors warned us about this form of government, yet we were never taught about this in school; we were fed just propaganda in our schools such as that we were a democracy. We are not, and we were never meant to be. Nor were we meant to be enslaved by socialism, but we have been enslaved in it by the deception of our Supreme Court, Congress, and president. Everyone has an opinion, but mine is that Roosevelt is the greatest traitor this country has ever had.

Again, the state governments have allowed the federal government to steal their authority without even so much as a grunt. This does not reflect well on the competence of our state governments, but this is the result of their not knowing our true history or our founding fathers' intent for the people.

All the laws our federal government have made regulating manufacturing and even safety in the workplace such as OSHA are illegal and violate Article 4, Section 1, the full faith and credit to the public acts clause. They also violate Article 1, Section 8, Paragraph 18, the true meaning of the powers necessary and proper clause that if properly titled would be the powers *vested by* clause and the Tenth Amendment stating power not granted to the federal government is reserved for the states.

I will finish up with the rest of Article 1, Section 8 by looking at the remaining powers that have been granted to Congress in my next article, Article 8. This is enough for one reading, and I want you to cogitate on what Natelson said. Talk to you in the next article. —March 27, 2015

Article 8: Shortcomings Part 3: Congress Continued

In Article 7, "Shortcomings Part 2: Congress," I discussed what powers our founding fathers had given Congress, and we looked at Article 1, Section 8, which enumerates the powers. In that article, I showed how Congress and the Supreme Court deliberately misconstrued the term *general welfare* in the first clause of Section 8 to usurp far more power than our founders intended to give to the federal government. I ended with a transcript of a clip I used of Professor Robert Natelson giving an explanation of how Congress and the Supreme Court neologize a definition of the word *commerce* to again illegally expand the authority of the federal government.

I will start where I left off, with the third supporting sentence of Section 8. Remember, I was indicating at the end of the sentence whether it was in support of the national defense portion of the first clause or the general welfare portion of the first clause. Sentence four reads, "To establish an uniform Rule of Naturalization, and uniform Laws on the subject of Bankruptcies throughout the United States" (general welfare).

Note there are two clauses in this sentence. The first concerns immigration laws, and the other regulates bankruptcies. Uniform rules and laws apply the same for each state; laws governing immigrants coming to live in Georgia apply to those coming to live in Pennsylvania and so on. The laws on bankruptcy apply in Ohio, Nebraska, and every other state. As a reminder, the Constitution was written by men who knew the literal meaning of words – the Constitution means what it says, and says what it means.

Sentence five reads, "To coin Money, regulate the Value thereof, and of foreign Coin, and fix the Standard of Weights and Measures" (general welfare). In this sentence, we have three clauses. I will look closely at this first clause, to coin money. Notice it states coin! This clause gives the federal government the authority to coin our money. To better understand what our founders meant by coin, we need to look at Article 1, Section 10, Paragraph 1.

> No State shall enter into any Treaty, Alliance, or Confederation; grant Letters of Marque and Reprisal; coin Money; emit Bills of Credit; make any Thing but **gold and silver Coin a Tender in Payment of Debts.**

As mandated by the Constitution, only gold and silver can be used as a means of currency. This means of payment can be changed only by an amendment to the Constitution. Do you remember what we learned from the court case *Marbury v. Madison*? This is one of those things no American should ever forget. Any law repugnant of the Constitution is void, and Congress lacks the power to increase or decrease powers granted by the Constitution. Congress has no power to make a law, act, or regulation changing this clause of the Constitution and make anything other than gold and silver the currency of the United States. It was the intent of our founding fathers that we would always be under a system of commodity money and for good reason. It is the only system that can provide economic stability. Do you notice that Article 1, Section 10, Paragraph 1 states, "no Bills of Credit are allowed to be emitted"? Bills of Credit is the old term for paper money. Paper money is actually illegal in this country.

The second clause of this supporting sentence gives Congress the right to mint money and to regulate its value. This means it can determine if an ounce of silver is going to be worth $1, $5, $10, and so on, and the same applies to gold. Congress can also determine the worth of foreign coins as well; they would determine this by the weight and purity of the precious metal in a coin.

The third clause allows Congress the power to set the standard of weights and measurements we use in the US. It was determined at the start of this nation to use English units of measurement, and it is still used in the private sector much today. But in 1988, with the Omnibus Trade and Competitiveness Act, Congress made the metric system the preferred unit of measurement when dealing with the trade of goods. This is the extent of the power given to Congress and the federal government by these clauses.

So how has our Congress and federal government abused these powers and violated the Constitution? First, they allowed the printing of fiduciary bills—paper money known as gold certificates and silver certificates. The certificate was to be equal in value to one gold or one silver coin, meaning that for every gold or silver coin minted, there was one gold or silver certificate printed to represent that coin. The idea was that paper money was easier to carry around than were heavy, bulky coins. And as you were able to redeem these certificates for the gold or silver they represented, they were considered as good as gold (or silver). Though the populace readily accepted them, there were three major problems with these certificates.

First, Congress lacked the power to make a law allowing it to make the certificates a legal means of tender as they were in violation of Article 1, Section 8, Paragraph 5 and Article 1, Section 10, Paragraph 1.

Next, it conditioned the people to accept paper money as a means of currency. Although this was precisely the plan, it was a horrible con job inflicted on the people.

Third, it had the effect that our founding fathers in their greater economic wisdom were trying to avoid. Banks were allowed to print these certificates; what they would do quite deceitfully was print up more than one certificate for each coin they had in their possession. They gambled that the people with the certificates would not redeem the certificates but would use them as currency as would the next person who received the bill. This way, they could lend money they did not really have and receive more interest. This is inflation, a way to steal from the people without their noticing.

But this was not the worst of it. In 1913, after the people had been conditioned to accept paper money, Congress passed the Federal Reserve Act. This act did two illegal things. First, Congress delegated its authority to regulate the value of money to a private financial institution called the Federal Reserve Bank. Sound like a conflict of interest? Second, it gave this institution the power to print fiat currency.

Fiat currency is paper money that has no true value; it has no gold or silver backing it. It is legal tender only by law. The problem with this is that Congress had no power whatsoever to legally enact such a law as it violated Article 1, Section 8, Paragraph 5 and Article 1, Section 10, Paragraph 1 of the Constitution. So in truth, the dollar bills you and I carry around in our wallets are actually worthless. We buy and sell things with them by total illusion. They have value only due to our uneducation and ignorance. I guess they are right when they say ignorance is bliss.

In addition to the Federal Reserve Act violating Article 1, Section 8, Paragraph 5 and Section 10, Paragraph 1, it also violates Article 1, Section 8, Paragraph 18, which is the powers vested by clause. (We'll get to that clause later in this article.) Remember, Congress lacks the power to increase or decrease the powers granted it by the Constitution including its own powers. By delegating its power to regulate the value of our money and putting it into the hands of a private financial institution without any oversight capabilities, Congress decreased its power and thus violated the Constitution. The Federal Reserve Act is unconstitutional and thus void; it also means that the Federal Reserve Bank is an illegal entity and therefore criminal in nature.

I have a question for you, and know, I don't have a definitive answer myself, just my opinion based on sound logic. If our multitrillion-dollar national debt is based on fiat currency, which is illegal and valueless, wouldn't that debt actually amount to nothing? Wouldn't all we have to do is recognize that it is ill-gotten gain, which a criminal is not allowed to keep or profit from, and it should all just go away? Vanish into the nothingness it actually is. This would make the rich men who paid off the senators who wrote and passed the act (for that is the only way such a law could have ever been passed) the poorest persons in this country. Everything they bought since 1914, when fiat currency was first printed, with this ill-gotten booty would be subject to confiscation.

There is a lot of criminal activity associated with the Federal Reserve Act. One crime I want to mention was committed by FDR. In 1933, he took us off the gold standard, which neither he nor Congress had the power to do without an amendment to the Constitution, and he asked the people to turn over their gold to the government to be replaced with gold certificates (Executive Order 6102 in 1933; remember that he had no such power). About 90 percent of the populace was gullible enough to do it. Then Congress backed his play by enacting the Gold Reserve Act of 1934. Then in 1935, FDR made it so Americans could not purchase gold. The promise was that they could get their gold back after the Great Depression was over. That never happened; the government kept all the gold. Not only is FDR the greatest traitor this nation has ever known; he is also the biggest thief.

So why the desire to create a fiat currency system? Fiat money is easy to inflate giving the controllers of the money the power to create depressions and recessions as they need or even create booms. In short, it is a means to become masters of the people. It is also a way to determine who is really in charge of this nation.

If these two clauses in the Constitution (Article 1, Section 8, Paragraph 5 and Article 1, Section 10, Paragraph 1) are not enough to convince you that only gold and silver coins are allow to be used as currency in this nation, there is also the next supporting sentence, Article 1, Section 8, Paragraph 6: "To provide for the Punishment of counterfeiting the Securities and current Coin of the United States" (general welfare).

Here, the Constitution grants Congress the power to make laws and set punishments for the counterfeiting of securities, basically US savings bonds, and for the counterfeiting of what? Coins. Again, the emphasis is on the commodity money of gold and silver. There is no allowance for Congress to make laws for the punishing of counterfeiting bills of credit (paper money) because they were never meant to be allowed in this country. So again, this clause in the Constitution gives Congress very limited power.

Although this next supporting sentence is relatively short, its two clauses give Congress a great deal of power to make laws on and for the establishment of multiple federal agencies, which it has done. Article 1, Section 8, Paragraph 7 states, "To establish Post Offices and post Roads" (general welfare).

I believe we're all familiar with the first clause, establishing post offices, and I'm not aware of any abuses of this clause. With the exception of some poor business practices in the past, I believe the federal government is doing pretty well with its management of the postal system. However, if it ever tried to do away with the federal post office, which can be done only by an amendment, it would also lose the power of the second clause as well, and that would be a big mistake.

The ability to establish post roads has given Congress the ability to establish the interstate highways we have and the US highway system as well. All other road systems belong to the states alone. This gives Congress the power to establish the Highway Transportation Department and make rules and regulations for driving on these post roads. It also has the power to enforce those rules by having federal officers patrolling the roads and issuing citations for traffic violations. I am surprised it has not already done this as it could be another source of revenue for it. As badly as Americans drive today, if the national debt were legitimate, it could be paid off in just one weekend.

All joking aside, this clause gives the federal government a great deal of power, and again, I do not know of any abuses of these clauses. Luckily, the states have used wisdom when granting the federal government the use of their lands for post roads to make them concurrent jurisdiction. I'll discuss more about that when I get to Paragraph 17.

The seventh supporting sentence of Article 1, Section 8 is another one of those clauses that the federal government has greatly abused and has usurped much of the states' authority and rights. Article 1, Section 8, Paragraph 8 states, "To promote the Progress of Science and useful Arts, by securing for limited Times to Authors and Inventors the exclusive Right to their respective Writings and Discoveries" (general welfare).

This clause has only two provisions. It gives Congress the power to set up a patent office and a copyright office and make the laws associated with both. This clause does not give Congress any other power. However, our Congress has done a very deceitful thing to steal the states' authority. They interpret the first portion of the clause as a separate clause and totally disregard the word *by*.

The word *by* is a limiting word restricting what Congress can do.

In this case, it limits Congress to only the power to promote science and useful arts through granting patents and copyrights. By ignoring the word *by* and creating new clauses where there are none, it has effectively stolen the rights of state governments. By making the new clause read "To promote the Progress of Science and useful Arts," it has made laws granting it the power to give school grants, finance museums, make laws regarding education, finance laboratories, and many other things that are the sole right of the state governments under Article 4, Section 1.

Many people might be inclined to say that all these things are beneficial, so where is the harm? First is the fact that these laws and programs violate the Constitution making them illegal. The intent of our founding fathers was to limit the power of the federal government and keep it in the hands of the state governments so we the people could keep a closer watch on things and have a greater say in the issues affecting our lives. By the federal government stealing this authority from the states, it has actually taken away this power from the people. Basically, it has candy-coated a dagger it has left in our backs.

The states also provide these same programs, so we are forced to pay more in taxes to pay for governmental redundancy. More government equates to more money out of our pockets that we could be spending on things we actually need and want thus stealing more of our choices and power.

By inventing the new clause so it could gain additional power, Congress violated the intent of not only this clause of Article 1, Section 8, but also the intent of Article 1, Section 8, Paragraph 18, Article 4, Section 1, and the Tenth Amendment.

The next supporting sentence is Article 1, Section 8, Paragraph 9: "To constitute Tribunals inferior to the supreme Court" (general welfare). This gives Congress the power to establish courts and judges subordinate to the Supreme Court. In the early years of this country, Congress established circuit court judges who rode horseback from state to state hearing cases involving violations of federal laws under the jurisdiction of Article 3, Section 2 of the Constitution. But Congress soon realized that this was too arduous a task for any man and decided to go with the district courts we know today. This was all we had until the late 1890s, when it was decided by the courts that they could not trust the judgment of juries and would not allow the people to be the final say in court cases. This was an unethical power grab by the courts. So in the 1890s, Congress added appellate courts to our judiciary system.

Article 1, Section 8, Paragraph 10, the ninth supporting sentence, consists of two clauses: "To define and punish Piracies and Felonies committed on the high Seas, and Offences against the Law of Nations" (general welfare). Any time you are on an American vessel or you are an American in your own vessel out on the open seas, you fall under the jurisdiction of the federal government. This gives Congress the authority to make whatever laws it deems necessary and proper for maintaining order over parties not on dry land. We call this maritime jurisdiction.

The second clause of this paragraph gives Congress the power to determine what punishments it feels are just for violations of international laws stemming from treaties. Remember though that in Article 6, Paragraph 2, all treaties made must be in accordance with the Constitution. If a treaty is in violation of the Constitution, no penalties for violating that treaty can be enforced.

This is a good place for me to stop for now as the next seven supporting sentences specifically explain what is meant by common defense in the opening statement of this section. I will need a whole article to explain those because a few of them plus the closing sentence have been violated by our federal government for well over a hundred years.

Think about what our founding fathers were intending when they penned the term *general welfare*. Always remember the intent of our founders; they wanted to keep us a free people, and the only way to keep us free is to limit the power we give our governments. They enumerated the general welfare powers of Congress so we would always know the extent of its power. They weren't being fickle when they wrote that Congress could collect taxes to provide for the general welfare, welfare being a public act, and then giving the states full faith and credit, authority, over public acts in Article 4. The general welfare they were talking about in Section 8 are services common to every state that were best handled by a central government. And truly this is all the power it should have.

So my next article will be the conclusion of what powers were given to Congress to make laws on.

—April 6, 2015

Article 9: Shortcomings Part 4: Congress, Conclusion

We are at part 4 on the "Shortcomings" series of these articles in which I discuss the authority given to the president and Congress by the Constitution. Doesn't really sound like it's all that short, does it? But remember, while I'm discussing what power is actually granted to our Congress and president by the Constitution, I'm also explaining many of the abuses of power by them as well, and our federal government is proficient at abusing the Constitution.

A major abuse I concentrate on is where they usurp the states' authority by giving the term *general welfare* a far broader and liberal meaning than the founding fathers ever intended it to have. When the term *general welfare* was scribed in the paragraph of Article 1, Section 8, it was meant as an introduction for the clauses that followed, not as an independent clause. The following nine sentences in Section 8 then described the actual limitation to what the founders were referring to as the general welfare. And it isn't what our modern Congress is claiming it is.

In this article, I look at the next seven sentences/paragraphs that are primarily concerned with what powers are given Congress for the support of our common defense.

The tenth supporting sentence of Section 8 may actually need a little extra defining as it uses some terms we don't use very often today. Article 1, Section 8, Paragraph 11 states, "To declare War, grant Letters of Marque and Reprisal, and make Rules concerning Captures on Land and Water" (common defense).

Only Congress has the power to determine if this nation will go to war with another nation. As we learned in my article "Shortcomings: The Presidency," the president can't perform his duty as commander in chief unless Congress gives him permission to do so. This was one of the proofs that the presidency is subordinate to Congress. Before the president can act, he has to call Congress together so it can vote on a war act so he can defend this nation. But after it has declared war, Congress's participation in defending this nation has almost ended. If Congress didn't add an appropriation clause to a war act, it would need to make an appropriation law supporting the war for at the most two years, and it would need to draft a letter of marque and reprisal, two words we don't hear very often, but every time we go to war, these are very important documents for the president to have.

Webster's 1828 dictionary defines a marque this way.

> Letters of marque are letters of reprisal; a license or extraordinary commission granted by a sovereign of one state to his subjects to make reprisals at sea on the subjects of another, under pretense of indemnification for injuries received. Marque is said to be from the same root as Marches, limits, frontiers, and literally to denote a license to pass the limits of a jurisdiction on land, for the purpose of obtaining satisfaction for theft by seizing the property of the subjects of a foreign nation. I can give no better account of the origin of this word.

Here's an example of how it works. During the Persian Gulf War, a letter of marque allowed our troops to use any captured supplies they might need including, say, food, gas, or vehicles without worrying about paying for them because they had the authority to take what they needed to fight the war. In short, it's a means for our troops to use the enemy's supplies to help us win the war, and it protects our troops from prosecution for doing so.

The last clause in this paragraph states that Congress has the power to make laws concerning captures (both people and property) on land and water. This is pretty much self-explanatory, so I am not going to spend much time on it here, but as of now, we send prisoners of war to Guantánamo Bay Naval Base in Cuba for safekeeping. Obama wanted to close this base for mindless reasons. I like the idea that if ever an enemy of this nation were to escape from a POW camp, he would not be in a position to harm US citizens. To me, this showed shortsightedness on the president's part as well as that of his supporters. Aren't they supposed to be protecting the citizens of this nation?

The eleventh supporting sentence/paragraph of Section 8 states, "To raise and support Armies, but no Appropriation of Money to that Use shall be for a longer Term than two Years" (common defense). So the US government can have an army, but Congress can secure money to support it for only two years. There is a good reason for that.

Tyrants have ever used their armies to force its laws on the people and keep them under control. Our founding fathers were well aware of this and wanted to safeguard the people from a rogue president. If a president ever abused his commander in chief role and started to use the army in ways he had no authority to do, Congress would just refuse to finically support the army and watch it fall into disarray. Not even the most simpleminded commander will follow the illegal orders of the president if he isn't going to be paid. The restrictive portion of this clause safeguards the people.

Article 1, Section 8, Paragraph 13 states, "To provide and maintain a Navy" (common defense). There is not the same restriction with the federal government maintaining a navy as there was with maintaining an army for two reasons. First, the navy is at sea and does not occupy land; this means it does not have the same resources as an army would need to maintain control over the populace. Also, all major invading armies would have to come by sea. This means you have to have an ever-vigilant navy to protect our shores while the army is rallied to counter any invasions of our beaches. And if your navy is good enough, the enemy fleet should never make it to our shores. Second, the navy has the full-time job of protecting our merchant ships from piracy.

Article 1, Section 8, Paragraph 14 states, "To make Rules for the Government and Regulation of the land and naval Forces" (common defense). This clause gives Congress the power to make laws that govern our military. We call these laws the Uniform Code of Military Justice; those of us who have been in the military call this the UCMJ.

The fourteenth supporting sentence in Section 8 states, "To provide for calling forth the Militia to execute the Laws of the Union, suppress Insurrections and repel Invasions" (common defense). Only Congress may make laws as to how and when the president is to ask the states to lend it their militia. This is another safeguard preventing a rogue president from gaining more control than he is allowed.

Look carefully at what is stipulated before Congress can call forth the militia. The first purpose is to execute the laws of the union. If there is lawless activity going on at some federal property such as rioting and looting, Congress can call forth the state militia to assist it in bringing back order to federal property or even have a state militia help another state with a problem.

Right after the Civil War, Union troops were left in the South to maintain law and order. These were the same troops that had just conquered the South, and the citizens of the Southern states were resentful of their presence. This was leading to open hostility by the Southerners. To keep the peace, Congress drafted and passed the Posse Comitatus Act, which prohibits the use of military forces to enforce laws in the United States. Can you see the problem with this act of Congress? It is in violation of this clause of the Constitution. Congress has no authority to create a law that violates or is repugnant of the Constitution; therefore, this law was always illegal. However, it was basically repealed by Executive Order 13528 by President Obama. Presidents have no authority to make laws; we covered that is my sixth article, "Shortcomings Part 1, The Presidency." But yes, President Obama did have the authority to declare the Posse Comitatus Act unconstitutional or in the case of Executive Order 13528 supersede the law because his oath of office mandated that. His oath of office gives a president the authority to void any act of Congress that violates the Constitution.

A very important thing to understand and notice is what military force is able to enforce national laws. The Constitution clearly states and specifies the militia, so only the military force that is ultimately controlled by a governor of a state can perform this act, not the regular US Army. Again, this is a safeguard to prevent an abuse of power.

The second reason given that Congress can call forth the militia is to suppress insurrection. Insurrection is what the South performed in 1861. So Congress had a legitimate reason to request the Northern states to supply the federal government with troops to squelch the insurrection.

Let's take a close look at the third reason that Congress can call forth the militia—to repel invasions. Here (and in Article 4, Section 4 for the same reason) is the only reason Congress has the authority to declare war on another nation. There is only this one reason given in this Constitution for when American troops can be called to go into battle in foreign lands. The standard by which Congress can declare war is whether there is a clear and present danger of a foreign army about to invade American soil. That is it. Because the Constitution does not grant any other reasons for calling forth the militia or engaging the regular US Army, this means Congress has no authority or power to engage our troops in battle but for these reason given—upholding laws of the union, insurrection, and invasion.

In the early 1950s, America troops were sent to Korea to fight for South Korea. Thousands of American troops died, and hundreds of millions of taxpayers' hard-earned dollars were spent. Was there any threat of invasion to American soil during this conflict? No. The conflict was designated a police action.

According to Article 1, Section 8, Paragraph 15, Congress can declare war and dedicate our troops only to repel invasions of this country. No clause in our Constitution gives Congress the authority to conduct world police actions, nor can any treaty be made that is repugnant of the Constitution. So any and all treaties made with any county or the UN stating that our country would supply troops for world police actions is unconstitutional as well and would be in violation of this clause of the Constitution.

As in Korea, the same thing happened in Vietnam in the 1960s and 1970s, the Iraq-Kuwait War in 1990, the Somalia War in the early 1990s, and still even more conflicts going on today in which American troops risk their lives in unconstitutional acts of war or police actions Congress had no authority to declare. This is a great reason all who consider themselves true Americans should fully understand the Constitution.

It is my opinion that every member of Congress and every president involved in these unlawful conflicts should be charged and convicted of war crimes. Don't get me wrong here; I have no contempt for our US troops who were forced to fight in these wars; they were obeying orders, and none was accountable for any wrongdoing. Our troops and sailors should be held only in the highest regard as the heroes they are. However, it's my belief that our legislative and executive branches should go to prison at the least.

Now that I've strayed from fact to opinion, it's a good time to get back on track and look at Article 1, Section 8, Paragraph 16. The fifteenth supporting sentence in this section states,

> To provide for organizing, arming, and disciplining,
> the Militia, and for governing such Part of them

as may be employed in the Service of the United States, reserving to the States respectively, the Appointment of the Officers, and the Authority of training the Militia according to the discipline prescribed by Congress. (common defense)

Sounds like Congress has a lot of authority over state militias, doesn't it? But this paragraph is amended by the first clause of the Second Amendment: "A well regulated Militia, being necessary to the security of a free State ... shall not be infringed."

As you can see by paragraph 16, the federal government has the responsibility to supply the states with guns, ammunition, tanks, and everything else they need to defend themselves. This paragraph also allows Congress to subjugate the militia to the UCMJ, both its laws and penalties. At the same time, it guarantees that the states will be responsible for appointing officers loyal to the state militias and that the states will train their troops, but the training has to conform to US standards. This makes sure that during a time of actual legal war, all American troops can perform in the same manner. It's good to have everyone on the same page on the battlefield.

The Second Amendment acknowledges the fact that the states' militia must be well regulated and Congress has the authority to bind them to the UCMJ. It also acknowledges that the federal government can take the lead when the nation is in a conflict where the militia is called up. The significance of the Second Amendment is that it ensures that state governments never relinquish their ultimate control over the militia; this is what "shall not be infringed" infers. If the governor of a state militia that has been called forth determines that the reason for the employment of his militia is unconstitutional, he has the power and right to recall his militia from the service of the United States. This is a right that the US government cannot transgress. This is another safeguard the founding fathers implemented to prevent the federal government from abusing its limited authority. Unfortunately, it is a states' right that has never been taken advantage of. Honestly, because of the uneducation of this nation, I don't think any governor in the United States understands this.

Also real quickly, notice that the Second Amendment states "free state." This is another reference to the fact that each state is its own sovereignty.

In the movie *Edge of Tomorrow*, a major who was busted down to private for desertion tells his new sergeant, "I see you're an American." The sergeant replies, "No, I'm from Kentucky." This is the perfect answer coming from a national guardsman. The first loyalty of an air or army national guard troop should be to his state and then to his country, the order of his allegiance.

Paragraph 16 is basically the last supporting sentence that deals specifically with the common defense referenced in the introductory sentence of this section. Did you see any reference to the federal government having and maintaining an air force? No. The air force was created by an act of Congress (the National Security Act of 1947). But what have we learned about the power of Congress to increase its authority? Remember *Marbury v. Madison*? Congress has no authority to increase its, or the president's, or the Supreme Court's power through an act, law, or regulation it passes. The president has no authority to increase the powers of Congress, the judicial branch, or his own. The judicial branch has no authority to increase the power of the legislative or the executive branch or its own. This power is not granted to any of the federal branches of government. For the US government to have an air force, there would have to be an amendment to the Constitution and the state governments would have to ratify that amendment. Only the states can increase or decrease the powers of the three federal branches of government. This is found in Article 5, Clause 3.

> ... for proposing Amendments, which, in either Case, shall be valid to all Intents and Purposes, as Part of this Constitution, when ratified by the

Legislatures of three fourths of the several States, or by Conventions in three fourths thereof, as the one or the other Mode of Ratification may be proposed by the Congress.

So what would this amendment look like? Quite simply, "Congress shall have the power to provide and maintain an air force." That is it. That is all Congress needed to do and then allow the states to ratify the amendment. In 1947, the states would have loved to give the federal government the authority to have an air force, but by 1947, Congress was so proficient at violating the Constitution that I doubt its members even knew how to function in a legal manner. They still don't.

Right now, under the Tenth and Second Amendments, only the states can have an air force legally as an air national guard. Because of the performance of the current federal government, it is clear to me that the states should never relinquish this authority to Congress or the president but should maintain the air force as an extra safeguard against tyranny.

The next supporting sentence of this section is actually a clarification of common defense and general welfare. Article 1, Section 8, Paragraph 17 states,

> To exercise exclusive Legislation in all Cases whatsoever, over such District (not exceeding ten Miles square) as may, by Cession of particular States, and the Acceptance of Congress, become the Seat of the Government of the United States, and to exercise like Authority over all Places purchased by the Consent of the Legislature of the State in which the Same shall be, for the Erection of Forts, Magazines, Arsenals, dock-Yards, and other needful Buildings.

What do these clauses state? An intelligent person would ask, "If the US government has eminent domain over this nation, why would it have to purchase or make a treaty with a state to obtain land? Wouldn't they already own it?"

The only land the federal government has any control over is its territories such as Guam, Puerto Rico, the Virgin Islands, and other such islands. Once a territory becomes a state, it becomes sovereign and controls all the land within its borders. This is guaranteed in Article 4, Section 4 as discussed in my earlier article. After a territory becomes a state, there are only two ways the federal government can obtain property in that state as mandated by this paragraph in Section 8: it can obtain this property by cession or by buying it. This section of this article is proof beyond question of the sovereignty of the states. What is meant by "by cession"?

> A yielding, or surrender, as of property or rights, to another person; particularly, a surrender of **conquered territory to its former proprietor** or sovereign, by **treaty**. —*American Dictionary of the English Language*, Noah Webster, 1828

For the federal government to obtain any property in its states, it must make a treaty with that state. It is solely up to the state legislature to determine if it wishes to give the federal government that land. There is no national eminent domain. It can offer to buy the land from the state, but that requires the state's permission; it cannot buy land directly from a private citizen or entity in that state.

This paragraph also puts strict limits on what the federal government can obtain land for—forts, (military bases), magazines and arsenals, (places to store munitions), dockyards, (naval bases), and other needful buildings.

To determine what is meant by needful buildings, we can look at the previous fifteen paragraphs and see what authority the federal government has to establish needful buildings—bankruptcy courts (paragraph 3), mints and possibly federally owned and operated banks (paragraph 4), post offices and post roads (paragraph 7), patent and copyright offices (paragraph 8), and federal courthouses (paragraph 9). This is it! These are the only things for which the federal government can purchase or make a treaty for land for.

I want you to look at something. This is a portion of the original ordinance that allowed Nevada to become a state.

ACT OF CONGRESS (1864) ENABLING THE PEOPLE OF NEVADA TO FORM A CONSTITUTION AND STATE GOVERNMENT

Section 4 Third. That the people inhabiting said territory do agree and declare that they forever disclaim all right and title to the unappropriated public lands lying within said territory, and that the same shall be and remain at the sole and entire disposition of the United States.

Applying what we just learned, was this act of Congress legal or unconstitutional? Let me give you some hints. The law is retaining the right to keep property as a condition of statehood, but that is in violation of Article 4, Section 4, and it is a clear violation of Article 1, Section 8, Paragraph 17. Congress cannot obtain land by an act but only by cession, treaty, or purchase. It cannot incorporate it into an act. This means that the government has no legal grounds to own all the land it claims in Nevada and every other state in the union that had such stipulations in its statehood ordinances; they are the true owners of the lands the federal government is now controlling. These ordinances are unconstitutional and therefore void. And according to Article 6, the states can and must declare them unconstitutional and simply take back control of the land.

I like our national forests and parks; I can hike through them, and enjoy other outdoor sports, without fear of trespassing on someone's private property, but all these lands are illegally claimed by the government and must be given back to the states.

If the government wants the states to set aside land for public forests, parks, wildlife reserves, grasslands, and agricultural lands, the only thing it can legally do is make a general law proving that such laws exist and the proof of the effectiveness thereof as outlined in Article 4, Section 1. This is exactly what that act should look like.

> In accordance with Article 4, Section 1, and in compliance with same said article, the United States Congress recognizes the fact that all of its citizens and the citizens of the several States have the right to enjoy the natural resources of this nation and the right to marvel at the diversity of wildlife and use these resources to their enjoyment. Congress is also well aware of the fact that its citizens and the citizens of the several States have the right to have an abundance of food to sustain them and for their enjoyment. In addition, Congress is well aware that the only way for the citizens of this nation, and of the several States, and their posterity, to enjoy these rights, that each State in this nation must set aside and maintain lands dedicated to these ends.

> Therefore this Congress is requiring each state in this union to present the laws they have enacted for the protection of public lands for the use of state forests, parks, wildlife preserves, and other public recreational land, and for the laws enacted dedicating lands for strictly agricultural use and needs not only for the present population, but for the future populations and citizenry. These laws will be presented to a congressional committee when Congress will next convene.

> This Congress will conduct a survey of the citizens of the several states to determine their satisfaction of the State public resources laws.

This is in complete compliance with Article 4 of our Constitution, and we are still assured public lands for our enjoyment. Everything we enjoy today can be enjoyed legally and in accordance with the Constitution if we would just apply it.

The last paragraph in Section 8 is a closing sentence establishing the limits to which the federal government can use its power. Article 1, Section 8, Paragraph 18 states,

> To make all Laws which shall be necessary and proper for carrying into Execution the foregoing Powers, and all other Powers **vested** by this Constitution in the Government of the United States, or in any Department r Officer thereof.

Now what our Congress, the president, and the judicial branch like to do is stop reading and acknowledging this clause at "all other Powers." Then they emphasize the terms *necessary* and *proper* as if that were the sole purpose of this clause. What they will never acknowledge is the rest of the clause, the true purpose of this clause, and that is "vested by this Constitution," which is the restraining portion of this clause. The purpose of this clause is to restrain and confine the federal government to the powers listed in the Constitution all of which are enumerated.

Many members of Congress and presidents have made the claim that if something is not prohibited by the Constitution, they have the right under the necessary and proper clause to do it. This is a bold-faced lie. This clause alone demands that all laws made by Congress and all departments, agencies, and offices in the federal government be in compliance with the Constitution. In addition, this clause mandates that all the powers granted to the officers of the United States, that is, the powers of all members of Congress, presidents, and judges, are limited by what the Constitution states those powers are. This is a restraining clause, not a "We can do whatever we want" clause, and this is not the only such clause as I have mentioned. Article 3, Section 2, Article 6, and the Tenth Amendment are other restraining clauses. Only through our national uneducation has our federal government gained such tyrannical powers. And it is going to get only worse.

All this deception, Congress's usurping the states' authority by illegally making laws controlling public acts and taking control of private industry by deceptive means, makes it clear that our federal government is no longer operating under the confines of the Constitution but is operating as a Marxist government. It is following the teachings of Karl Marx to the letter. Actions speak louder than words.

I'd be willing to say that nearly 90 percent of the laws and agencies now under the federal government are unconstitutional and thus criminal in nature. But it had to do this. With the limitations placed on it by the Constitution, Congress would have passed all the laws necessary to run the federal government two hundred years ago. And it did. It should have stopped making new law two hundred years ago and convene for only a short time just to pass appropriation bills. But it has become a full-time professional legislature, so it had to swear to uphold the Constitution with one breath and violate it with the next. There is no way for a free people to remain free with a full-time professional legislature. Just can't happen. And there is nothing more pathetic than a nation of slaves who think they're free.

In my next article, I will address what our founding fathers were trying to establish when they wrote the Second Amendment. It is a lot more than you think. I am titling it "Armed or Not to Arm."
—April 6, 2015

CHAPTER FIVE

ARTICLES 10-11

Article 10: Armed or Not to Arm

In the last four articles, my "Shortcomings" series, I introduced you to the powers and authority granted to the president and Congress as well as the limitations placed on them by the Constitution. We started off by going step by step over Article 2, Sections 2–3, looking at what the president was actually supposed to be doing and at the tremendous amount of limitations set in place to restrain that authority. I also showed how the last several presidents abused that authority by ignoring these restraints and acted criminally in doing so. Any intentional violation of the Constitution is a crime.

After I explained the true role of the presidency, we looked at the powers and authority as well as the limitations of Congress. In those articles, I showed you how our government was abusing its authority and ignoring those limitations. I even showed what murderous results were caused by its total disregard of this document its members have sworn upon oath to support.

What I haven't explained is why or how this contempt for the Constitution came about; how did our federal government become so corrupt? Some scholars will tell you that this is just a natural process of government. Malarkey! Considering the way the Constitution was laid out, the abuses we see so prevalent today could never have happened if the Constitution was just adhered to. But when you closely examine our history and by applying reasonable logic, it becomes quite clear that there are two major reasons this corruption manifested. I will discuss one reason in this article and the second in the next.

If you have a constitutional republic as we are supposed to have in America, a governing body out there is guaranteed to destroy that republic and subjugate its citizens to slavery. By its very nature, it has no other recourse but to make slaves of the people. What is this governing body? It is a full-time professional legislature. I am not exaggerating here. A full-time professional legislature can have only one result—the enslavement of its people.

When a constitution places limits on the authority and responsibility of its government as our Constitution does, there will naturally come a time when laws needed to proficiently run the government will be made. When you have a limited number of things you can make laws on, there is a limited number of laws you can make. Simple logic. Because of this, there comes a time when the best thing a legislative body can do is admit that no additional laws are required except for an appropriation bill and adjourn the congressional session. There is no way for a full-time professional legislature to do this; its members have to make laws even if there is no need for new laws. Otherwise, there would be no reason to have a full-time professional legislature, and its members would be out of cushy, low-expectation jobs. Once legislators get a taste of jobs that require them to sit around deliberating and on rare occasions doing the arduous task of raising their hands to vote yea or nay on a bill, they become very reluctant to give up such jobs. And look at all the great perks. You can give yourself a raise any time, pass laws that are binding on and detrimental to the people while making yourself exempt, you can take bribes—Oops, I mean campaign contributions—and you can get a full pension after one term. Not to mention an exclusive health care plan and travel benefits. This is the reason states that don't have full-time professional legislators are constantly having their legislatures trying to pass laws making them full-time. This is never a good thing. As we can see in the example of our federal government, this is rotten.

It was not very long before Congress made all the laws necessary for conducting the business of the federal government, but by that time, Congress had made itself a full-time profession. It must find ways to expand its authority so it has the power to make new laws to keep itself in business. Congress has no legitimate authority to gain additional power except by amendments to the Constitution, which the states must ratify. Many amendments have been presented by Congress; the states have passed very few but still more than they should have. I have already discussed various methods Congress with the aid of the Supreme Court has deceptively and illegally added powers for themselves, so I won't reiterate them.

It was never the intention of the founders that being a member of Congress would be a full-time job. Because of the hardships of travel in 1787, the writers of the Constitution believed that the majority of those in the Senate and House would want to perform their civic duty only once. That is what the founding fathers considered governmental service; it wasn't thought of as a way to make a buck. This is very apparent when you examine the wording of the Constitution; Article 1, Section 4 states that Congress is to assemble at least once a year, and Article 1, Section 6 states that senators and representatives shall receive compensation instead of a salary. This was why in Article 1, Section 3 that the Senate was originally divided so that a third would be elected two years apart from the other two-thirds so as to always have seasoned senators to guide the new ones and why Congress was to meet in the dead of winter, which was the hardest time for travel for anyone those days. It was so they could be back at their farms and plantations for planting and harvesting. No, there was no intent for members of Congress to have full-time positions, but with the advent of the steam engine, travel became easier and so did the job of legislating.

So now we have a federal legislation that is constantly violating the Constitution and regularly usurping the states' authority. With full-time professional legislators, it couldn't happen any other way. All they can do is make excessive laws that strip the people of their rights and enslave them.

But is only our federal government violating the Constitution? What about the states? Are they adhering to the Constitution as they are required to under Article 6? Every time they turn their back on an unconstitutional law passed at our nation's capital and do not denounce it but rather enforce it, they violate the Constitution. And the states themselves are passing laws that violate the Constitution.

Let us take a look at the Second Amendment.

> A well regulated Militia, being necessary to the security of a free State, the right of the people to keep and bear Arms, shall not be infringed.

I already discussed the purpose of the first clause of this amendment in my ninth article, "Shortcomings Part 4, Congress, Conclusion," and how it ensures that states have ultimate control over their militias even when they have been called to service by the U.S. government. It also confirms that states may have military forces so they can defend themselves. This is the security a militia brings the state. The founding representatives of Nevada understood this when they wrote Article 1, Section 11 of the Nevada State Constitution.

> Right to keep and bear arms; civil power supreme.
>
> 1. Every citizen has the right to keep and bear arms for security and defense, for lawful hunting and recreational use and for other lawful purposes.

Notice that it states the purposes, and first on the list is security and defense. I want to point out that it states that the civil power is supreme. This means of course that the power of the citizens is supreme over the power of the state militia. This is another way of calling this power a privilege and immunity of the citizens of the state. Back to the purpose. The Nevada State representatives understood that the rights to have a militia and keep and bear arms were primarily for the purpose of defense.

It's the second clause of the US Constitution's Second Amendment that I want to address, "The right of the people to keep and bear Arms, shall not be infringed." What is this clause all about? Why did the founders of this nation deem it so important that they amended the Constitution to contain it?

Robert Natelson, the constitutional law professor I have mentioned before, discussed the Second Amendment; in his presentation, he made the assertion that one, the Supreme Court in the 5–4 Heller decision, (District of Columbia v. Heller 2008, Heller, a special policeman for the District of Columbia was denied a registration by the district to keep a handgun in his home.) declared that the Second Amendment did constitute an individual right but that the historical documentation was not clear on this point. Two, Natelson said that the Bill of Rights did not originally pertain to the states but only to the federal government. The belief that any of the Bill of Rights applied to the states was a new, twentieth-century doctrine coming out of Congress, but again, only certain portions of the Bill of Rights apply to the states, not all of them. Is our scholar right in anything he had to say? Let's look at the Constitution.

Natelson stated that there was not enough historical documentation to be sure of this amendment's meaning. I disagree. What is the one historical document we can always use to determine the meaning of the Constitution? The Constitution itself. The only reason you would need to look for external constitutional documentation is if you didn't like what it has to say and you're looking to find someone else's opinion that supports yours.

Let's look at the second half of this amendment; remember our eighth grade English. Notice the comma after the word *State*.

It's signifying that the same idea, self-defense, is implied but a different subject is addressed—the right of the people. It can't get any plainer than this. This second clause of the Second Amendment is undoubtedly addressing private citizens, not the militia. Yet our Supreme Court ruled 5–4 ruling that the comma did imply that this was a protection of an individual's rights to keep and bear arms. Wouldn't this imply that four of the nine Supreme Court justices didn't have even an eighth-grade education?

The next assertion Natelson made was that the Bill of Rights was never intended to apply to the states. Basically, he was asserting that the Bill of Rights was a document separate from the Constitution, but as I wrote in my fifth article, "The Rights of the States Part 2," there is no Bill of Rights; that was just a name applied to the first ten amendments that were ratified in 1791, the key here being that they were ratified. Ratified amendments become part of the Constitution according to Article 5; they are not separate laws to be treated in any manner differing from the Constitution. So this is the second thing on which our scholar was wrong.

Next, he asserted that the Second Amendment was never intended to apply to the states, but Article 6 clearly states that the Constitution is the supreme law of the land making all laws written at every level of government subject to it, and it clearly states that "the judges in every State shall be bound thereby, anything in the Constitution or laws of any State to the contrary notwithstanding." This clearly subjects the states to the authority of the Constitution as well. The states derive their authority from the Constitution in Article 4, and Article 5 applies to the states as well as the federal government; limitations of the states are spelled out in Article 1, Section 10 of the Constitution. The Second Amendment applies to the states as well as to the federal government and always has. There are just not enough people today who are properly educated to understand this document anymore, especially our scholars.

Were our founders acknowledging our right to wear weapons merely as a fashion statement? No. The purpose of this article far exceeds that. But first you need to understand what the Second Amendment is—a right. Most people believe that if they like doing something, they have a right to do it. That's not quite true; that's called license, "excessive or undisciplined freedom." Even our Constitution does not grant us license. When the Constitution was written, the founding fathers understood a right this way.

> Right, Conformity to the will of God, or to His laws, the perfect standard of truth and justice. In the literal sense, right is a straight line of conduct, and wrong a crooked one. Right therefore is rectitude or straightness, and perfect rectitude is found only in an infinite Being and His will. - *American Dictionary of The English Language*, Noah Webster, 1828

The best modern definition I've been able to find is this: "That which is just, morally good, legal, proper, or fitting. In accordance with fact or truth" – *The American Heritage Dictionary of the English language 1976*. Not everything we are allowed to do in this country is a right. For instance, abortion was made legal via illegal case law even though it is immoral and unethical.

Our founding fathers were very gracious to us in that they didn't give us our rights but secured them as well as various privileges for us. Today, we call the Second Amendment a right. The founders would have called it a privilege and an immunity. Many Americans today have been led to believe that they are granted their rights by the government and that the rights we have are spelled out in the Bill of Rights. This is just not so. The Bill of Rights was not drafted to give us our rights but to protect them from the governments. Most people don't realize this, but the first Bill of Rights this nation ever had, and it is still in effect, is the Declaration of Independence. It established the United States as an independent, sovereign nation, defined the character of this nation, and defined where our rights were derived from. In this country, our rights are God given. This is good because what God gives, no mere man or government can take away. But if our rights are granted by the government, the government can take away those rights. Any sane person would be terrified at the prospect of the government having that much control.

A right is an act conforming to a perfect standard of truth and justice based on moral integrity. If what you are doing is morally correct, you have a right to do it. One more thing you should know about rights. For every right or privilege and immunity you have, you have duties and obligations. You don't get one without the other. When laws are made, they should be to enforce the duties associated with the right and not the right itself.

To what extent are our rights protected? Did you notice that just above, I called our protected rights privileges and immunities? I got that out of the Constitution. This is how our founding fathers defined our rights, and every word in the Constitution has a specific purpose our governments must abide by. You find the term *privilege and immunities* in Article 4, Section 2, Paragraph 1: "The Citizens of each State shall be entitled to all **Privileges and Immunities** of Citizens in the several States."

The 14th Amendment, Section 1, reads,

> All persons born or naturalized in the United States, and subject to the jurisdiction thereof, are citizens of the United States and of the State wherein they reside. No State shall make or enforce any law which shall abridge the **privileges or immunities** of citizens of the United States ...

To understand the degree of protection the Constitution gives us, we need to understand the definition of the words *privilege* and *immunity* that our founding father knew. In Webster's 1828 dictionary, we read that a privilege is any peculiar benefit or, right or **immunity**, not common to others of the human race. Thus we speak of national privileges, and civil and political privileges, which we enjoy above other nations. We have ecclesiastical and religious privileges secured to us by our constitutions of government. Personal privileges are attached to the person.

Immunity is defined as an

e**xemption** from any **Charge**, **duty**, office, **tax, or imposition**; a particular privilege; as the immunities of the free cities of Germany; the immunities of the clergy.

This is the degree of protection we have in the Constitution. If we are exercising any one of our protected rights, the government cannot charge us with a crime and cannot impose any fee or tax for exercising our rights; nor can we be sued for exercising our rights. Our government is just not given the power to do anything to infringe or violate our rights, and any violation of our protected rights is a criminal act by the government(s).

Now that you know what the Second Amendment is, let's examine what privilege and the extent of that privilege you have immunity on.

You are given the right to keep and bear arms, and this right cannot be infringed upon. Let us use again Webster's 1828 dictionary to get the clearest picture of what our founding fathers' understanding of the words *keep* and *bear* mean so we can ascertain to what extent this protection protects us. There is a full page of meanings for the words *keep* and *bear* in this dictionary. Obviously, our founding fathers had a vastly greater comprehension of our language than our scholars of today do, but the definition of the word *keep* that applies here is this.

1. To hold; to retain in one's power or possession; not to lose or part with; as, to keep a house or a farm; to keep any thing in the memory, mind or heart. 2. To have in custody for security or preservation.

We are the ones to have power over our own possessions, not the government.

The definitions of *bear* that apply here are these.

2. To carry; to convey; to support and remove from place to place; as, 'they bear him upon the shoulder;' 'the eagle beareth them on her wings.' 3. To wear; to bear as a mark of authority or distinction; as, to bear a sword, a badge, a name; to bear arms in a coat.

Look again at this last definition. Notice how it says to bear arms in a coat. You guessed it; the Second Amendment is really our license to carry concealed weapons. You have to understand that the politicians 225 years ago were vastly more intelligent than today's politicians. They understood that self-defense weapons were worn usually on a belt. And of course, in colder weather or as fashion might dictate, you would most likely put on a coat thus concealing your weapons. It is just common sense, and the debate about being allowed to carry a concealed weapon would have been ludicrous to our founding fathers, who expected it.

A person arms himself to defend himself, his family, his belongings, his livelihood, and others who might not be able to defend themselves. Do you see any limitations on the types of arms with which you are allowed to defend yourself within this immunity? No, you don't. That is because you may carry any form of weapon you choose to defend yourself, and no government can make any laws prohibiting you from carrying it. You have immunity. Can you carry your weapon concealed? Yes! A woman may carry her handgun in her purse, or a man may wear a weapon strapped to his waist and cover it with a jacket without any condemnation from any government official.

Let us look at the last portion of this amendment: "... shall not be infringed." This is not a suggestion. It is a command. Who is it commanding? All levels of government. What is meant by *infringed*? Webster's dictionary defines it this way.

> 1. To break, as contracts; to violate, either positively by contravention, or negatively by non-fulfillment or neglect of performance. A prince or a private person infringes an agreement or covenant by neglecting to perform its conditions, **as well as by doing what is stipulated not to be done**. 2. To break; to violate; to transgress; to neglect to fulfill or obey; as, to infringe a law.

To give you a clearer picture of what this entails, let me compare it to a similar word that is used in real estate. That word is *encroached*. Encroachment is an unauthorized invasion or intrusion of an improvement or other real property onto another's property. Exempli gratia, if you and your neighbor have driveways along the same property line and one day your neighbor parks his trailer in his driveway in such a way that just the corner of the bumper of that trailer crosses over onto your driveway, your neighbor has encroached on your property. Just the smallest breach is all it takes. If your neighbor refuses to move his trailer after you ask him to, he has committed trespass, and you can seek a judicial remedy.

This is exactly like an infringement in law. Even the slightest breach of a protected right is a trespass on your right and a criminal act on the part of the government. In short, it is a crime for any legislative body (federal, state, county, or city) to make a law that violates or infringes on your right to defend yourself. It is also a crime if the courts even hear a case much less render a judgment against you in a case concerning a protected right such as the Second Amendment.

No government can make a law prohibiting you from carrying the self-defense weapon of your choice either openly or concealed, and you cannot be arrested or sued for using your weapon in self-defense.

Let me give you some examples of how this works. Clark County, Nevada, had a law requiring citizens who owned handguns to register them with the county. Was this law legal? No! First of all, it was infringing on the citizens' right to keep arms. Second, no government entity has the right to know what you or I legally own or possess. According to the Constitution, the only way a government agency can determine what I possess is through a warrant, and the only way it can get a warrant is if it can show probable cause that I committed a crime. It is legal, not a crime, for me to own a handgun under the Second Amendment. So this law is also in violation of the spirit of the Fourth Amendment of the Constitution and therefore void.

I'm an amateur historian, and this law violates every fiber of my being as I am well aware of what happened to the citizens of Poland and Czechoslovakia when Nazi Germany invaded those countries during World War II. Both required their citizens to register their guns, and the first thing the Germans did was go to the police stations to get those registration forms so they could confiscate the guns or kill their owners. There is no legitimate reason for a government to have its citizen register their weapons. Oh they may state some reasons, but not one has any validity.

In Las Vegas, you can carry a dagger or dirk as long as it is carried openly, but in Henderson, Nevada, which is separated from Las Vegas by just a street, it is illegal to even carry a dagger or dirk. Think about it. One minute you are legal and the next minute just by crossing a street you are illegal. This is some of the mindless stupidity that our founding fathers were trying to avoid when they drafted the Constitution. So was either the Las Vegas law or the Henderson law legal? No, neither! The Las Vegas law infringes on your right to bear arms as obviously did the Henderson law. Neither municipality has the power to violate the Constitution as they are both bound by its Article 6.

In Las Vegas and Henderson, it is illegal to possess a bludgeoning weapon, a stick or club used to strike someone. I for one am very fond of a bludgeoning weapon as I am very adept in its use and know the psychological effect it has on people. While I was a uniformed police office, there was more than one occasion when I placed someone under arrest prior to my backup getting there that a suspect asked after I informed him that I was arresting him, "Yeah? You and what army?" That was literally the line they used. That of course is the wrong thing to say to a police officer as it gives him the authority to go to the next level of force to accomplish his job, and for me, per agency policy, that was my baton. In all the times I had a tough guy challenge me, not once did I have to clear my baton from its ring before the suspect consented and said, "Sir! I'll do whatever you ask! Just don't hit me with that stick!"

The beauty of a bludgeoning weapon is that you can use it in various levels of force. You can brandish it at threating persons to let them know you have the ability and intent to defend yourself, or you can apply controlled strikes to a person to stop an attack, or you can apply deadly force when all else fails. One thing I want you to recognize—all these actions are protected under the Second Amendment. You can take any level of action you deem necessary to protect and defend yourself.

The key to applying the Second Amendment as it relates to defense is that you feel threatened for your safety or the safety of another. As long as you are being threatened and you fear for your safety, you can take whatever action and use whatever weapon you are comfortable with to defend yourself. This includes using a weapon to take the life of your attacker. As long as there was an obvious threat, you cannot be arrested, prosecuted, or even sued for defending yourself or your household.

To what extent does the Second Amendment protect you from prosecution or lawsuit? A while back, a court case involving a burglar made the news. The burglar broke into the garage of a home by dropping through the roof. Once inside, the burglar found that the resident had protected his home by putting padlocks on all the doors of the garage, and the burglar could not get out. The owner of the home was gone for a number of days before he came home to find the burglar there; he had the police come to arrest him.

During that time, the burglar had only some dog food and soda pop that was in the garage to sustain him. The burglar sued the homeowner because he had been trapped in the home with little sustenance. And believe it or not, the idiot judge awarded the burglar restitution. Did the judge have the authority to even hear the case? No. The homeowner has the right to defend his property by any means possible, and that includes putting padlocks on his doors. The Second Amendment even covers cases like this. This is how important this immunity and privilege is and the extent by which it protects us.

Some lawmakers have made laws restricting certain types of weapons such as switchblades, batons, etc. because they believe they give someone an unfair advantage over another. This type of thinking is the product of someone who has lead a cushy life and has never gotten into a fight. When you are forced to defend yourself, there is no such thing as an unfair advantage. The entire purpose of carrying weapons is to give you the advantage over your attacker. Police officers carry many weapons on their utility belts so they can always have the upper hand in a physical confrontation. The same holds true for the average citizen. The only person who can have an unfair advantage in a fight is an aggressor who arms himself for an attack. The person on the other end of the attack is forced to react to what he sees, putting him at a disadvantage. So having one of those weapons that some uneducated and highly unenlightened lawmaker made illegal might be the very thing that would have saved his life.

Can lawmakers make such laws? No. To do that, they would have to abridge your Second Amendment privilege and immunity, and lawmakers disdain this limitation. Quite literally, the Second Amendment prohibits any laws at any level of government—federal, state, county, or municipal—involving your having a self-defense weapon on your person or in your household, and all such laws are unconstitutional and therefore illegal.

Can any laws be made concerning weapons? Yes! The Second Amendment and so many state constitutions' privileges and immunities apply only to defensive weapons, not offensive weapons. When is a weapon an offensive weapon? Any time you commit a crime, you are in an offensive posture, so any weapon you have on you becomes an offensive weapon and you can be charged with the crime of possessing an offensive weapon. Also, if you become angry and pull your once-defensive weapon for an attack, that weapon becomes an offensive weapon and you are no longer protected by the Second Amendment.

It does not matter what type of weapon you have on your person; what matters is how you are using it. As long as your sole intent for your weapon is to use it in defense of yourself, your family, your home, or another person being attacked, it is legal for you to have and use it and no court or cop can say differently. However, if you commit a crime with a weapon on your person even if you have no intent of using it, it is an offensive weapon and you have no legal protection. You can be arrested and charged.

I stated earlier that with every right come duties and obligations. Laws also can be made to enforce your responsibilities as a gun owner. The one law I could justify for state governments to make (as they deal with public acts and is the states' right under Article 4) is that before you are allowed to purchase a gun or any projectile weapon or the ammunition for those weapons, you have to have completed a weapons safety course and given a certificate showing you have completed the course. States cannot make laws requiring you to have a safety certificate as a stipulation to carry the weapon as that would breach your Second Amendment privilege and immunity. But as the gun and ammunition are not yours prior to your purchasing them, they can make laws requiring you to show that you know how to safely use it prior to your obtaining it. The law shows you have taken the steps needed to prove that you know your responsibility concerning the safe handling of weapons.

A quick test. Can you shoot your neighbor's pit bull that is charging you? Yes. It's an obvious threat and you are defending your safety. Can you discharge your weapon as part of a New Year's celebration? No. This would be a careless discharge of your weapon. If a girl is on a date and the boy tries to force himself on her to the point that she pulls a boot knife she had concealed under her pant and stabs his leg, can she be charged with assault or sued? No. She has every right to carry a concealed weapon, and if she feels her safety is threated, she has every right to use that weapon to ward off that threat. The key is that she felt threatened. That is all it takes to defend yourself.

One pet peeve I have is when people state guns kill. My retort to that statement is, "Yes, but they also save lives." At that, most liberals go into convulsions because you have challenged their limited ability to think. If someone is standing over you ready to plunge a knife into your chest and a police officer shoots him off you, has not the gun just saved your life? If a soldier uses his rifle to stop an advancing enemy, has not the gun just saved his life and the lives of his fellow soldiers? If a man is in the forest and is forced to shoot a charging grizzly bear, has not the gun just saved his life? If a man is injured in the forest and he uses his gun as a signal to aid his rescuers in finding him, has not the gun just saved his life?

A gun is nothing more than a tool that can supply enjoyment as a recreational sport, save lives, or murder and cause mayhem. What makes the difference is the mind-set of the person using the tool. If the person using the tool is healthy minded, well adjusted, and honorable, the tool will be used for good. But if the person using the tool has a depraved mind, you will have murder and mayhem. And this is why the statement that guns kill is such a pet peeve of mine. It is because it points away from the true problem of society, and this mindless misdirection prohibits us from ever addressing the real issues. When you put the blame of an abased society on guns and do not address the real issues, the real issues can never be resolved and therefore murder and mayhem continue to spread. Those placing all the world's problems on the tool and not addressing the real issues are more to blame for the depravity of our society than even the ones committing the murder and mayhem.

So what is the real issues we should be addressing? What is causing our society to become so vile and abased? Do you understand cause and effect?

In the 1950s, the worst offense a student committed was chewing gum in the classroom. In the 1960s, though they had no authority to do so, the federal courts took prayer out of our schools. Today, we have mass murders, drugs, cyberbullying, and armed guards in our schools.

Starting in the 1960s, our federal courts started removing the Ten Commandments from our courthouses. Again, they had no authority to do so. Today, murders are set free after serving just a few years in prison just to murder again on a regular basis. The federal courts legalized murder in the form of abortion, and now, women are murdering their newborn babies or even older children because they have become a nuisance. Our crime rate has soared, and people are in constant threat of having their identities stolen, and so many other problems. Has anyone ever noticed the connection? The more we push God out of our society, the more-depraved and vile our society becomes. And this is why liberals would rather point their fingers at guns rather than address the real problem.

—April 11, 2015

Article 11

NATIONAL CHARACTER

In my Article 10, "Armed or Not to Arm," I stated that there were two main reasons this nation's governance has become so corrupt. The first as you may recall was the result of having a full-time professional legislative body, a bad idea for any people who cherish freedom. In this article, I explain the second reason our government has become so corrupt.

In addition, we will be looking at Amendment 1 of the Constitution as it is directly related. But before I can do that, I need to be sure you understand the type of character our founding fathers expected the people of the United States to have. And yes, they did have the right to expect the progeny of this nation to maintain this high standard of moral cognizance. So what was the countenance this nation was expected to wear?

Did you know that the Declaration of Independence is the most important of our laws of the land?' One time when I was a young federal law enforcement officer on a special detail, a group of us were discussing laws. The Declaration of Independence was brought up, and a rookie officer who was a college graduate said, "The Declaration of Independence really has no significance. It was written only as a morale booster for the soldiers at Valley Forge." I and the other three older officers who came from military police backgrounds looked at him as if he were joking, but he was not. One officer asked him, "If it isn't significant, why is it in a place of honor in all federal buildings?"

Many federal buildings have a display of the laws of our land in their lobbies, and the Declaration of Independence is always placed in the top center position with the Constitution and Bill of Rights below and on either side. This is the position of honor indicating that it is the most important of the documents.

The young college graduate officer could only repeat what he said earlier. Another officer asked him, "Then what makes us a country?" Our college grad answered, "The Constitution." Someone asked him, "Then what were we between the time the Declaration was signed in 1776 and the Constitution was adopted in 1789?" As any good college graduate who is faced with a question that disproves his indoctrination, he simply walked away.

I did not even get to ask him my question, which would have been, "If the Declaration was signed in 1776 and the winter of Valley Forge was December 1777 to February 1778, how the founding fathers foresee the need for a morale-boosting memo? Did they have a crystal ball? If they had that foresight, why didn't they arrange for food, warmer clothing, better shelter, and ammunition? Wouldn't that have been a better morale builder than a memo?"

The Declaration of Independence is the most important law this country has. Why would a college law professor program his students to think differently? The vast majority of our college campuses and professors are primarily liberal minded and lean toward socialism. Of course a good Socialist clings to the teachings of Karl Marx, and Marx's teachings are the complete antithesis of the five principles the Declaration of Independence establishes.

First, it declares this nation to be an independent and sovereign nation.

> When in the Course of human events, it becomes necessary for one people to dissolve the political bands which have connected them with another, and to assume among the powers of the earth, the separate and equal station to which the Laws of Nature and of Nature's God entitle them.

Socialists have no problem with this principle; it just means they have a country rule, but the mention of God unsettles them.

The second principle established by the Declaration is the

character by which this nation was to be known. It was to run under Christian principles, and it confirms that our rights are God given.

> We hold these truths to be self-evident, that all men are created equal, that they are endowed by their Creator with certain unalienable Rights, that among these are Life, Liberty and the pursuit of Happiness.

Socialists have a big problem with this. Karl Marx taught,

> Where the political state has reached its true form, man leads a double life, a heavenly life and an earthly one, not only in thought, in consciousness, but in reality, in life itself. He leads a life within the political Community ... The political state is as spiritual in its relation to civil society as heaven is in the relation to earth. —Karl Marx, Question on the Jewish faith Bruno Bauer's critique

This is the religion that our government, the Supreme Court, Congress, and the presidents have established for the American public to follow. So a document that refutes this Marxist religion needs to be marginalized or defamed.

The third principle that the Declaration of Independence establishes is that the people are the true authority of this nation and that the government is subject to them.

> That to secure these rights, Governments are instituted among Men, deriving their just powers from the consent of the governed.

Of course this is the complete antithesis of what the Marxist religion mandates, which is that the people are to be the slaves to the state and are to worship the government.

The forth principle established by the Declaration of Independence is also a right protected by this document—the right of the people to remove government officials injurious to our way of life.

> That whenever any Form of Government becomes destructive of these ends, it is the Right of the People to alter or to abolish it, and to institute new Government, laying its foundation on such principles and organizing its powers in such form, as to them shall seem most likely to effect their Safety and Happiness ... But when a long train of abuses and usurpations, pursuing invariably the same Object evinces a design to reduce them under absolute Despotism, it is their right, it is their duty, to throw off such Government, and to provide new Guards for their future security.

As you can see, this is not just a right protected; it is also a duty of the people. Again, this is not a very popular concept with Socialists. The thought of their being replaced by the people because of their corrupt practices—How dare they!

The fifth principle established was a list of reasons a people would have a right to remove themselves from an established government or replace their civil servants. As our present government violates nearly all the listed grievances and others not on the list, this is definitely not something liberals would want you to learn.

The Constitution is an extension of the Declaration of Independence, and the first thing our founding fathers did when they penned it was to expound on the third principle of the Declaration, that the people were the true authority of this republic. The preamble of the Constitution states,

> **We the People** of the United States, in Order to form a more perfect Union, establish Justice, insure

domestic Tranquility, provide for the common
defense, promote the general Welfare, and secure the
Blessings of Liberty to ourselves and our Posterity,
do ordain and establish this Constitution for the
United States of America.

Notice how it starts off with "We the People." I have talked
about the Declaration of Independence a number of times in past
articles and the relevance it has to this nation still today. Indeed,
between the Declaration of Independence and the Constitution, the
Declaration of Independence is the more substantial and influential
of the two documents to the people of this nation, or it should be.
This is why it is in the place of honor when displayed in federal
buildings. When the founding fathers wrote the Declaration of
Independence, what was the character ascribed to this nation? As
stated above,

We hold these truths to be self-evident, that all
men are created equal, that they are endowed by
their Creator with certain unalienable Rights,
that among these are Life, Liberty and the
pursuit of Happiness.--That to secure these rights,
Governments are instituted among Men, deriving
their just powers from the consent of the governed.

Of course this is just a portion of the Declaration of
Independence, but it is sufficient to depict the character that we as
patriotic Americans should have. First, we are to acknowledge that
God is our Creator and that our rights are derived from Him, and
next, we are to cherish our freedom and our right to secure a good
life. Was it the intent of our founding fathers that we should be a
Christian nation? If so, how important was it for us to maintain
these principles to ensure our freedom? To answer these questions,
we need to look at the writings of the men who established and

nurtured this nation so we can understand their beliefs and intents. Read carefully and ponder intently to determine for yourselves the importance of Christianity in American politics.

> The general principles on which the fathers achieved independence were the general principles of Christianity, Now I will avow that I then believed, and Now believe, that those general principles of Christianity are as eternal and immutable as the existence and attributes of God. —John Adams

> Statesmen, my dear Sir, may plan and speculate for liberty, but it is Religion and Morality alone, which can establish the principles upon which freedom can securely stand. —John Adams

> We have no government armed in power capable of contending in human passions unbridled by morality and religion ... Our Constitution was made only for a moral and religious people. It is wholly inadequate to the government of any other. —John Adams

> To preserve the government we must also preserve morals. Morality rests on religion; if you destroy the foundation, the superstructure must fall. When the public mind becomes vitiated and corrupt, laws are a nullity and constitutions are waste paper. — Daniel Webster

> The great pillars of all governments and of social life are, virtue, morality, and religion. This is the armor ... and this alone, that renders us invincible. —Patrick Henry

On the mercy of my Redeemer I rely for salvation and on His merits; not on the works I have done in obedience to His precepts. —Charles Carroll

Without morals, a republic cannot subsist any length of time; they therefore who are decrying the Christian religion ... are undermining the solid foundation of morals, the best security for the duration of free government. —Charles Carroll

I entreat you in the most earnest manner to believe in Jesus Christ for "there is no salvation in any others" Acts 4:12. KJV If you are not reconciled to God through Jesus Christ, if you are not clothed with the spotless robe of His Righteousness. You must forever perish. —John Witherspoon

I am constrained to express my adoration of ... the Author of my existence in full belief of ... His forgiving mercy revealed to the world through Jesus Christ, through Whom I hope for never ending happiness in a future state. —Robert Treat Paine

I subscribe to the entire belief of the great and leading doctrines of the Christian religion ... and I exhort that the way of life held up in the Christian system is calculated for the most complete happiness that can be enjoyed in this mortal State. —Richard Stockton

My only hope of salvation is in the infinite transcendental love of God manifested to the world by the death of His Son upon the cross. Nothing but His blood will wash away my sins. I rely exclusively upon it. Come Lord Jesus! Come Quickly. —Dr. Benjamin Rush

In contemplating the political institutions of the United States, I lament that we waste so much time and money in punishing crimes, and take so little pains to prevent them. We profess to be republicans and yet we neglect the only means of establishing and perpetuating our republican forms of government. That is, the universal education of our youth in the principles of Christianity by the means of the Bible. —Dr. Benjamin Rush

The only foundation for ... a republic is to be laid in Religion. Without this there can be no virtue, and without virtue, there can be no liberty, and liberty is the object on life of all republican governments. —Dr. Benjamin Rush

Christianity is the only true and perfect religion; and that in proportion as mankind adopt its principles and obey its precepts, they will be wise and happy. —Dr. Benjamin Rush

I ... rely upon the merits of Jesus Christ for a pardon of all my sins. —Samuel Adams

Let divines, and philosophers, statesmen, and patriots, unite their endeavors to renovate the age, by impressing the minds of men with the importance of educating their little boys and girls, of inculcating on the minds of youth the fear and love of the Deity ... in short, of leading them in the study and practice of the exalted virtues of the

Christian system. —Samuel Adams, in a letter to John Adams, October 4, 1790

Religion and good morals are the only solid foundation of public liberty and happiness. —Samuel Adams

Rendering thanks to my Creator ... for my birth in a country enlightened by the Gospel ... to Him I resign myself, humbly confiding in His goodness and in His mercy through Jesus Christ for the events of eternity. —John Dickinson

To the triune God - the Father, the Son, and the Holy Ghost - be ascribed all honor and dominion for - evermore - Amen. —Gunning Bedford

I believe that there is one only living and true God, existing in three persons, the Father, the Son and the Holy Ghost ... and that at the end of this world there will be a resurrection of the dead and a final judgment of all mankind when the righteous shall be publicly acquitted by Christ the Judge and admitted to everlasting life and glory, and the wicked be sentenced to everlasting punishment. —Roger Sherman

Unto Him who is the author and giver of all good, I render sincere and humble thanks for His manifold and unmerited blessings, and especially for our redemption and salvation by His beloved Son ... Blessed be His holy name. —John Jay, Original Chief Justice to the Supreme Court

Religion is the only solid basis of good morals; therefore education should teach the precepts of religion, and the duties of man towards God. — Gouverneur Morris, one of the writers of the US Constitution

In my view, the Christian Religion is the most important and one of the first things in which all children, under a free government ought to be instructed ... no truth is more evident to my mind than that the Christian Religion must be the basis of any government intended to secure the rights and privileges of a free people. —Noah Webster

The moral principles and precepts contained in the Scriptures ought to form the basis of all our civil constitutions and laws ... All the miseries, and evils which men suffer from vice, crime, ambition, injustice, oppression, slavery, and war, proceed from their despising or neglecting the precepts contained in the Bible. —Noah Webster

Of all the dispositions and habits which lead to political prosperity, religion and morality are indispensable supports ... In vain would that man claim the tribute of patriotism who should labor to subvert these great pillars of human happiness, these firmest props of the duties of men and citizens. And let us with caution indulge the supposition that morality can be maintained without religion ... reason and experience both forbid us to expect that national morality can prevail in exclusion of religious principle. —George Washington, in his Farewell Address

This is just a small sampling of the writings of the men who signed the Declaration of Independence and the Constitution or had an impact on the early development of this nation. Think about what each of these men had to say. Did you notice the recurring theme, that the Christian religion was an indispensable part of the running of this nation? Yet modern historians, or more correctly, liberal revisionists, have written articles with titles such as *The founding fathers Were 'Not' Christians* by Steve Morris, *Authors of the Declaration Were Enemies of Christ* by Bob Massey in the *Sun Herald*, *The Godless Constitution: The Case Against Religious Correctness* by Isaac Krumnick and Laurence Moore, and in the *LA Times*, an article titled *Americas Unchristian Beginnings*, which opened with, "Founding fathers—most, despite preaching of our pious right— were deist, who rejected the divinity of Jesus."

Do any of these articles or books match up with the quotes of the founders you just read? Absolutely not. So why the blatant lies? There has to be a reason for them. Why would the liberal left want Americans to believe that we were never meant to be a Christian nation? What do they gain by it?

When the founding fathers established this nation as a Christian nation, they intended that we acknowledge God as our sovereign and abide by the principles laid out by Him and not for us to be a theocracy.

Not only are these christophobes revisionists maligning our founding fathers; they are also attacking the foundation of the Christian faith as well, that being the Bible. A PBS presentation was aired a little while ago supposedly presenting archaeological evidence of how the Bible and its new monotheistic religion actually came about. They started on the premise that the Bible was not true as it is written and then came up with their own preconceived notions as how it actually came about. Then they looked at archaeological findings and asserted that the findings matched the preconceived notions. They found statues of cows and women with babies and concluded that these were idols worshipped by the Hebrews first, and then they developed a monotheistic religion later disregarding what the Bible said about idol worship. Ever notice how archaeologists always try to find significance in everything they find? Never once did the idea that the sculptures could be nothing more than decorative figurines such as those found in many modern homes today enter their minds. Kind of like petroglyphs; could they be nothing more than some ancient adolescent's graffiti?

Regardless, their premise was faulty. The Bible presents itself as an eyewitness account of history. As any good investigator knows, you must first accept a witness's statement as true and then corroborate and substantiate the statement or discredit it with physical or additional documental evidence.

So what these storytellers did (I won't honor them with the title scientists) is equivalent to a criminal investigator bringing a case before a judge and saying, "Your Honor, we had to tamper with the evidence and misrepresent what it indicates, and then we had to rewrite our witness's statement to match our version of the physical evidence, or otherwise you would never find the defendant guilty of what we are charging him with." Just as this is bad police work, it is just as bad scientific reporting.

So are we being deceived by what the Constitution says about religion? Let's take a look at Amendment 1 of the Constitution to see what our founding fathers said about religion.

> Congress shall make no law respecting an establishment of religion, or prohibiting the free exercise thereof; or abridging the freedom of speech, or of the press; or the right of the people peaceably to assemble, and to petition the Government for a redress of grievances.

The First Amendment represents what our founding fathers called a privilege and immunity and what we call a protected right today. We are interested only in the first two clauses right now though the third, fourth, and fifth clauses are closely intertwined with the first and second clauses. Again, the first two clauses read, "Congress shall make no law respecting an establishment of religion, or prohibiting the free exercise thereof." These clauses are addressing Congress because only the legislative branch is permitted to make laws. The first clause prohibits Congress from establishing a national religion or endorsing the states' establishing state religions. That is why the word *respecting* was used. In England and other European nations, kings mandated what religion would be practiced in their kingdoms. The founding fathers were addressing this practice.

Do you see the phrase *freedom of religion* in this or the second clause? The second clause states that no laws can be made that prohibit the free exercise of our religion, but does this clause protect all religions? Remember what a right is—a choice based on a moral and ethical decision. When you read the writings of the founding fathers in regard to the protection of religion, they always used the phrase *of good conscience* associating it with that protection. Therefore, only religions that are founded on the principle of the betterment of humankind can be deemed as protected by this amendment. Therefore, logic dictates that a religion that is inherently detrimental to society such as Satanism would not be protected by this clause. Again, you have to have at least an eighth-grade education to understand the Constitution.

Do you see anywhere in this clause the phrase *separation of church and state*? No! That is because it is not there. Yet when our federal courts discuss religion, they refer only to the First Amendment as the separation of church and state.

When our founding fathers wrote, "no law respecting an establishment of religion," what was their definition of *establishment* as used in this sentence? Webster's dictionary of 1828 defines *establishment* as "the act of establishing, founding, ratifying or ordaining." Okay, to cover our bases, let us see what the definition of *establishing* as the founders knew it was: "Fixing; settling permanently; founding; ratifying; confirming; ordaining."

In any of these definitions, do you see anything vaguely similar to separation of church and state? So where did our courts come up with this terminology that they use to control religion? Well, it is not from the Constitution. It was derived from a letter written by Thomas Jefferson to the Danbury Baptist Church in 1802. So the courts are basing their opinions on the opinion of one man, not the Constitution. Bad judgment. But what was the opinion of Thomas Jefferson? And are our courts rendering a proper interpretation of Jefferson's opinion? Let's look at Jefferson's letter. But before we do, we must first look at the letter from the Danbury Baptist Church Jefferson was responding to so we may understand his response. Because of its length, I am going to give only the portion of the Danbury letter Jefferson was addressing in his letter. I have highlighted important concepts for you to take note of.

> Our Sentiments are uniformly on the side of Religious Liberty - That Religion is at all times and places a matter between God and individuals - **That no man ought to suffer in name, person, or effects on account of his religious Opinions -** That **the legitimate Power of civil government extends no further than to punish the man who works ill to his neighbor**: But Sir our constitution of government is not specific. Our ancient charter together with the Laws made coincident therewith, were adopted on the Basis of our government at the time of our revolution; and such had been our Laws & usages, and such still are; {t}hat Religion is considered as the first object of Legislation; and therefore what religious privileges we enjoy (as a minor part of the State) we enjoy as favors granted, and not as inalienable rights; and these favors we receive at the expense of such degrading acknowledgements, as are inconsistent with the

rights of freemen. **It is not to be wounded at therefore; if those, who seek after power & gain under the pretense of government & Religion should reproach their fellow men - should reproach their chef Magistrate, as an enemy of religion Law & good order because he will not, dare not assume the prerogatives of Jehovah and make Laws to govern the Kingdom of Christ.**

Sir, we are sensible that the President of the United States is not the national legislator, and also sensible that the national government cannot destroy the Laws of each State.

The fear of the Danbury Church was that because the federal government broached the subject of religion in the First Amendment, the government would assume that it could make laws governing religions. This was Jefferson's response to that fear in its entirety. Again, I highlighted key phrases.

To messers. Nehemiah Dodge, Ephraim Robbins, & Stephen S. Nelson, a committee of the Danbury Baptist association in the state of Connecticut.

Gentlemen

The affectionate sentiments of esteem and approbation which you are so good as to express towards me, on behalf of the Danbury Baptist association, give me the highest satisfaction. My duties dictate a faithful and zealous pursuit of the interests of my constituents, & in proportion as they are persuaded of my fidelity to those duties, the discharge of them becomes more and more pleasing.

Believing with you that religion is a matter which lies solely between Man & his God, that he owes account to none other for his faith or his worship, **that the legitimate powers of government reach actions only, & not opinions**, I contemplate with sovereign reverence that act of the whole **American people which declared that their legislature should "make no law respecting an establishment of religion, or prohibiting the free exercise thereof," <u>thus building a wall of separation between Church & State.</u>** Adhering to this expression of the supreme will of the nation in **behalf of the rights of conscience**, I shall see with sincere satisfaction the progress of those sentiments which tend to restore to man all his natural rights, convinced he has **no natural right in opposition to his social duties.**

I reciprocate your kind prayers for the protection & blessing of the common father and creator of man, and tender you for yourselves & your religious association, assurances of my high respect & esteem.
—Th Jefferson, Jan. 1. 1802

In a nutshell, Jefferson was saying that government should not infringe upon the business of the church, not that the church shouldn't influence the government as it is being interpreted today. Jefferson himself made treaties with Native Americans allowing and supporting missionary work. Also, Jefferson would sign all laws presented to him and all other official government document by adding, "On this date in the year of our Lord Jesus Christ," invoking the name of Jesus in every government document.

According to the christophobic community, Thomas Jefferson was a deist, but would a deist do such things as he did? Obviously,

Jefferson was not stating that the Christian religion should be abolished from every sphere of government. He was stating that the government, federal or state, had no business making any laws or hearing any cases in which religion was concerned. Notice that Jefferson stated that the legitimate powers of government reached actions only, not opinions; laws were to address wrong behavior, not belief. Our government was not to be our moral guide. Yet the only thing the federal courts have focused on for the last eighty years is the phrase *separation of church and state*. Is there a reason for this? Let's take a quick look at the history of the concept of the separation of church and state and see if we find a pattern. Let's go back to pre-FDR and the New Deal era and look at the Scopes trial.

The American Civil Liberties Union (ACLU) went looking for someone to refute the Butler Act of Tennessee, which prohibited the teaching of evolution. Understand this—by 1927, science had long debunked Darwin's theory. It would be resurrected only by communism under Vladimir Lenin for reasons I'll explain later. So why would a union or the ACLU want to promote Darwinism?

They found a teacher, John Scopes, willing to make the case. The ACLU used the First Amendment and applied the phrase *separation of church and state* to it as part of its defense. Initially, it won the case, but it was appealed to the Tennessee Supreme Court and was overturned on a technicality. In its opinion, the Tennessee supreme court said,

> We are not able to see how the prohibition of teaching the theory that man has descended from a lower order of animals gives preference to any religious establishment or mode of worship. So far as we know, there is no religious establishment or organized body that has in its creed or confession of faith any article denying or affirming such a theory.

What an insightful observation. Notice that this case did not go any further than the Tennessee supreme court. This is because the

Constitution dictates in Article 4, Section 1 and Article 3, Section 2, Paragraph 1, that only state governments may hear cases between a state and the citizens of the state. Let's look at some post-FDR and New Deal–era court cases.

In the 1947 case *Everson v. Board of Education*, a christophobe complained about public transportation being used for religious schools. The Supreme Court stated, "The First Amendment has erected a wall between church and state. That wall must be kept high and impregnable. We could not approve the slightest breach."

However, the court did rule that public transportation could be used for religious schools as these families were taxpayers as well.

In 1962, the Supreme Court in *Engel v. Vitale* eliminated state-sponsored prayer.

> For this reason, petitioners argue, that State's use of the Regents' prayer in its public school system breaches the constitutional wall of separation between Church and State. We agree with that contention, since we think that the constitutional prohibition against laws respecting an establishment of religion must at least mean that, in this country, it is no part of the business of government to compose official prayers for any group of the American people to recite as a part of a religious program carried on by government.

In 1963, in *Murray v. Curlett*, the Supreme Court ruled to abolish school prayer and Bible reading stating, "Religious freedom, it has long been recognized that government must be neutral and, while protecting all, must prefer none and disparage none."

In 1968, the Supreme Court ruled in *Epperson v. Arkansas* that the Arkansas law prohibited the teaching of evolution violated the establishment clause of the First Amendment. It said the clause prohibited the state from advancing any religion. At this time, the court said schools should give equal time to alternative theories.

In 2005, the US Court of Appeals Sixth Circuit ruled in *ACLU v. Mercer County* (Kentucky) that the Ten Commandments could be displayed as part of a larger display of American legal tradition in the courthouse. The display was secular and meant as educational. But in 2006, a federal judge ruled that the Mount Soledad cross needed to be taken down because it was on public property.

In 2005, federal judge John E. Jones III ruled that the Dover school board had violated the Constitution when it set its policy on teaching intelligent design stating,

> **In making this determination we have addressed the seminal question of whether ID (intelligent design) is science.** We have concluded that it is not, and moreover that ID cannot uncouple itself from its creationist, and thus religious, antecedents.

This is just a small sampling of the federal court cases using the separation of church and state as a means to abolish Christianity from our society. No other religion in America has come under such attacks, and Islam seems to have additional privileges that no other religion has. Special concessions have been made in the public arena to support Islam with total governmental support. This fact would seem to nullify the separation of church and state argument the courts give, wouldn't it?

What are some other problems with these post-FDR New Deal–era court cases? The first clause of the First Amendment states that Congress shall make no law respecting an establishment of religion. Are displays and statues laws? Is supporting a moral religion the same as establishing a religion? The answer is no to both questions. Yet to any objective observer, there is obviously a war being waged against the Christian religion. What is the purpose? Is the separation of church and state the true intent of the courts and our governing officials?

In practice, in reality, what form of government is practiced here in the United States of America? It is not democracy; it never has been though—hint hint—we are constantly being told we are a democracy. Give this some serious consideration. What did Professor Natelson say about our government when he was talking about commerce? He said,

> This Constitution was written for a relatively small government. It was not written for a government that controls thirty sum odd percent of the American gross domestic product. Okay! So when the people complain of the unresponsiveness of the Congress, or the arrogance of bureaucrats, or the level of the taxes, or whatever, **you have to keep in mind this is largely a product of the fact that we have taken a form of government that is designed for a mostly free people and changed it into a government that regulates virtually every aspects of our lives.** That was not what the government was set up to do. So you get all kinds of problems.

Here are a couple more facts to help you determine what form of government is practiced here in America. Did you know that when he established communism in Russia, Lenin legalized homosexuality and abortion? (See Black, *When Nations Die*, in references.) He also established no-fault divorce and established universal, free health care. Everything that communist Russia established we have established here in the United States after the FDR administration. What was the New Deal? Simple. Marxist socialism.

Go back to my first article and recall the various forms of governments I talked about. Which one do we most closely resemble? If your conclusion is a fascist nation, you're correct. Everything we are practicing today was practiced by the Nazi party under Adolf Hitler during World War II. (See Halbrook, "Registration: The Nazi

Paradigm" in resources.) This nation parallels the progression of the rise of socialist power in Germany from the late 1800s through the reign of Hitler. So why then the war on Christianity?

To understand that, you have to look to the author and architect of communism, Marx. All three forms of Marxist socialism (socialism, fascism, and communism) subscribe to the theory of Marxism. So what did Marx say about religion?

> Where the political state has reached its true form, man leads a double life, a heavenly life and an earthly one, not only in thought, in consciousness, but in reality, in life itself. He leads a life within the political Community ... The political state is as spiritual in its relation to civil society as heaven is in the relation to earth. —Karl Marx, Question on the Jewish faith Bruno Bauer's critique

Marx was saying that the state and the government must become the god of the people. That's right; politics was Marx's and his followers' religion.

Our courts or government have no intent to create a separation of church and state; their intent is to establish a religion, that of Karl Marx. You can't have two competing religions in a society especially when one, Marxism, requires the total slavery of the people and the other, Christianity, preaches freedom of the people; the two religions are at odds with each other. This is why we see so many attacks on Christianity in our courts and by our lawmakers today. This is also why Lenin resurrected Darwin's theory of evolution; evolution does away with the need for God Jehovah.

Is there any real empirical scientific evidence that supports evolution, or does it support the Creator of the universe as the founders of science such as Newton, Boyle, Kepler, and Galileo believed? Let's take an honest look at the scientific evidence.

THE FOSSIL RECORD

Evolutionists state that the fossil record clearly establishes evolution. Does it? All fossils found are of fully formed animals and plants. There are no transitional fossils to be found. To prove Darwin's theory, you would have to find the thousands of transitional animals it would take for a fish to transform into a lizard. You read that right. Thousands of morphological changes are required to go from a fish to a lizard, yet not one has ever been found. The same is true for a man to evolve from an ape. As of today, all transitional pre-human beings have been frauds. What was thought to be a Neanderthal man found in the late 1800s near Düsseldorf, Germany, was just a human with arthritis.

Also, if animals have been living on this planet for the hundreds of millions of years as the evolutionists claim, there would be trillions of fossils all over the world. Give it some thought. If man went from a few thousand to seven billion in just four thousand years, how many dinosaurs must have lived and died in those hundreds of millions and even billions of years? Even if most decayed away, we should still dig up a dinosaur every time we dig in our garden. But that doesn't happen.

In addition, the vast majority of fossils are found in coal mines. This is why we call them fossil fuels. The only way for all those fossils to have gathered in the same place at the same time and then be produced into coal is if a massive flood happened and washed them to those locations and the water was deep enough to produce the type of pressure needed to transform organic material into coal.

The empirical evidence supports the Bible and Noah's flood rather than evolution. Evolutionists say that the mass extinction of the dinosaurs came about as the result of a meteorite strike. They fail to state that the gases and heat created by this meteorite that killed the dinosaurs would have killed all the other living creatures as well and that nothing evolves from extinction. Early miners brought canaries into the mines with them because birds are highly susceptible to poison gases and would die at the first sign of them. A dead canary meant get out fast. These are the same gases that were supposed to have caused the extinction of the dinosaurs. So every time you see a bird, it is proof that their demise was not by a meteorite strike but by a flood.

Does astronomy and the big bang theory support evolution or creation? The physics shows that at one point at the creation of all things, there was nothing. Evolutionists claim that an unknown force instantaneously created all matter. Christians call that unknown force God.

DATING OF FOSSILS

Carbon 14 dating is one of the most accurate forms of dating fossils, but what evolutionists fail to tell the public is that carbon 14 has a half-life of a little over 5,700 years and that after 100,000 years, there would not be enough Carbon 14 in a fossil to get a reading. As all fossils tested have had carbon 14, and the amount that is found means that all life that ever existed on this planet has been here less than 50,000 years. Helium diffusion dating places the earth at about 6,000 years old, the same as the Bible.

Evolution is not science; it is religious dogma. And every Marxist stands behind it with a fervor and devotion that an Islamic suicide bomber would envy.

It is important to note here that every one of the court cases post-FDR and the New Deal era and every other case concerning religion, evolution, abortion, and civil rights heard by the federal courts since are in violation of Article 3, Section 2; Article 4, Section 1; Article 4, Section 4; Article 1, Section 8, Paragraph 18; Article 1, Section 1; and the Tenth and Eleventh Amendments of the Constitution or any combination thereof. The courts have no authority to hear a case or appeal from a case involving a state and a citizen of that state or a state and citizens of a different state or nation. The courts have no authority over cases involving public acts, no court can breach the sovereignty of a state and make rulings on whether a state law is constitutional, no law or act can be made granting more power to the courts, the courts have no power to make laws, and no court can breach the authority of the states. This means that these cases are all unconstitutional and therefore void.

The reason we see this war on the Christian faith here in the United States and the rest of the world isn't to separate religion from politics; it is to establish the Marxist religion of politics. Our Constitution was designed to protect us from this one-world religion, and it allows us to believe what our good conscience and good sense dictate.

This might be the most diabolical plot against the people the Marxists have as it separates the people from their true God and salvation, but it is not the only malevolent scheme they have. I'll show you something almost as horrible in my next article.

—April 29, 2015

ARTICLES 12-14

Article 12: Subterfuge and Solution Part 1

I'm sure my last article and especially my conclusion was a jaw-dropper for most of you, and right about now, you're thinking, *This guy must be some kind of a radical, conspiracy-theory nutcase.* But remember what I said and asked you at the start of these articles; I said I'd be teaching things that would go against your core beliefs and worldview and asked you to be open minded when judging the material by the evidence I provided and for you to research what I said for yourselves. I have provided the proof to go with everything I have said so far.

If the revelation that our government is manipulating our culture to profess the religion of Karl Max through chicanery was unsettling enough for you, you're going to have a real hard time digesting the first half of this article.

We all want to feel safe with our government, to feel that our government is really looking out for the best interests of the people. Even I want that. But I am a realist, and I see things for what they are, not the way I want them to be. If you believe that our government is truly looking out for our best interest, make a quick study of the rise of the Third Reich. Note the attacks on the Christian faith, the social policies put in place by Hitler and his cohorts, and how Hitler used the courts to legislate when the legitimate legislation was too slow or uncooperative. Then compare what you learned with what you observe going on in this nation. It is my belief that as long as you're honest with yourself, you will see history repeating itself. But I wonder how well you've been taught our history.

Have you noticed that when it comes to teaching about the early European settlers that the compacts and charters they made and other original writings of the earliest settlers have all been altered in school history books? Their compacts have been altered to take out any reference to God and their religious intent. Our national leaders such as George Washington are maligned as was done in W. E. Woodward's book *George Washington, The Image and the Man* (1926). Woodward claimed in his book that Washington was a godless deist and an immoral man, but never did he note where his information was derived from. Nothing in his book is supported by the historical writing during Washington's life or by what Washington himself wrote. But modern history textbooks cite Woodward's book as their source document. Lies upon lies. In John Fredric Schroder's 1855 book *The Maxims of George Washington*, he inserted written testimonies of historical figures such as John Marshall and Elias Boudinot, who knew Washington and attested to Washington's Christian faith. Yet when that book was recently republished, it was revised by replacing all the testimonies with commentaries by college professors who claimed that Washington was a deist. Why would they do this? What benefit does it bring?

In 1831, Alexis de Tocqueville, a French lawyer, came to America to try to determine why America was such a flourishing and prosperous nation and had become so in such a short time. After four years of studying America, in 1835, he wrote a book on his conclusions; his title for the book, *Democracy in America*, was slightly off; it should have been *Republicanism in America*. He wrote that the obvious success of America was due to its people's strong

Christian faith. A third of his book explains how Christianity was the overwhelming catalyst for America's success. Yet again in a revisionist, abridged version of *Democracy in America*, every reference to the influence of Christianity was deleted. Why? What was the purpose of eliminating our heritage?

Ever notice how today's policy makers and college professors insist that we are a multiple cultural nation? Notice how we are always allowing immigrants into this nation and then catering to their cultural beliefs? We don't seem to expect them to adapt to our culture; we make concessions to them. Why this emphasis on cultural diversity? Here is a clue to the answer to that question. Remember that our leaders are practicing fascism and are Marxist. So whose teachings should we look to to understand this emphasis on making this nation a multiple cultural nation and denying our heritage? What does Karl Marx have to say about the subject? "A people without a heritage are easily persuaded."

Marx was not merely making an observation here; when Marx wrote, he did so to instruct. He was instructing good Communists on how to gain control of the populace and to subvert them into communism. Think about it; any group of people who have been around two to three hundred years have a heritage. America's heritage was started a little over five hundred years ago. In 1492, Columbus sailed the ocean blue. So how can Marx say people without a heritage are easily persuaded? He is instructing good Communists to alter the past to give the populace the revisionist history they need to manipulate the masses to believe what they want them to believe.

Give it a little thought; how would you go about destroying others' heritage to make them believe that their ancestors actually viewed life in a fashion totally different from the way they actually did? If you can make people believe that their ancestors believed in one set of values, you can make them believe they should hold that same set of values. People are simple that way, or should I say easily persuaded. To go about destroying a populace's heritage, wouldn't you first want to rewrite history eliminating any inference to a set of morals that are contrary to what you want them to believe? Then would you not want to debase the noble character of their founders to reflect a character closer to your own, or worse, so you could persuade them not to follow in those founders' footsteps? Then would you not ignore all the good your country did and teach only about the weakness of the country or its less inspirational moments in history? Is this not exactly what the liberals are doing now and have done to this nation?

All nations have regrettable moments in history. People are only human and prone to make mistakes. The key is that they corrected those mistakes and learned from them. Our nation did just that. But liberals just keep looking into our dark past to persuade you and me that we should think like them. The irony is that the decedents of the liberals are the ones who influenced all the mistakes this nation made. As the saying goes, the more things change, the more they stay the same.

I am going to give you another of Marx's teachings, and I want you to figure out for yourself how you would go about bringing this teaching to fruition.

> A particular social sphere must stand for the notorious crime of society as a whole so that emancipation from this social sphere **appears** as general self-emancipation. For one class to be par-excellence the class of emancipation, another must conversely be the obvious class of oppression. — Karl Marx, Contribution to the Critique of Hegel's philosophy of right.

Do you understand what Marx was teaching? In layman's terms, keep the people at odds with one another and they will become dependent on government. You must first get one segment of society to believe that it is inferior to another segment (such as minorities vs. the majority) and then make the inferior segment (the class of emancipation) feel the need to free itself from that superior segment of society (the class of oppression). Notice Marx used the word *appears*. There does not necessarily have to be any real oppression; you just have to suggest there is oppression and people will liberally join the bandwagon. And why would you do this? To gain control over of the minds of the people. If you control what people think, you control the people. They become your slaves.

So how would you achieve this goal? Remember, you're going to have to do this slowly and over a long period. If you move to quickly, the people might notice what you're doing and revolt.

So have you figured out how you are going to subjugate the people under your control yet? This is not going to be easy to write as I am going to scrutinize the Civil Rights Act of 1964. This act has a special place in many Americans' hearts, and there is much that can be speculated on in this turbulent time in America's history. I am going to touch on only the surface of this period.

The act was drafted by President John F. Kennedy. Does a president have the authority under the Constitution to draft a bill? No. Only Congress can draft bills and make laws. So from the very get-go, the Civil Rights Act was illegal. But do I question the president's intent? Kennedy is one president I'm not sure about when it comes to his genuine concerns about the people. And two of his stated constitutional reasons for his bill were equal protection under the law under the Fourteenth Amendment and protection of voter rights under the Fifteenth Amendment, both just reasons for a legitimate civil rights law at the time.

His third supporting clause he tried to use was Article 1, Section 8, Paragraph 3 dealing with commerce, but he was applying the New Deal–era Supreme Court definition, which is totally unconstitutional, thus making Kennedy's civil rights bill in violation of the Constitution and violating the very clause he was citing that was supporting his bill and making it again illegal.

Kennedy was absolutely right when he felt the need to use the federal government's power under Article 4, Section 1, Paragraph 1, "the Congress may by general Laws prescribe the Manner in which such Acts, Records and Proceedings shall be proved, and the Effect thereof,' to force state, county, and municipal governments to fulfil their obligation under Article 6 and abide by the Fourteenth and Fifteenth Amendments. But the law needed to be in compliance with the Constitution.

As it is, the Civil Rights Act violates Article 4, Section 1 because it violates both the full faith and credit to the public act and the general laws clauses of the Constitution as it was way too specific and not general in its nature; Article 1, Section 8 because it violated the true intent of the commerce clause; Article 1, Section 8, Paragraph 18 because it went beyond the authority of the federal government; and Article 1, Sections 1 and 7 because it violated legislative authority by Kennedy drafting the bill.

At that time, Congress should have drafted a civil rights act that forced the states and lesser governments to comply with the Constitution, but that is as far as it should have gone. As it is, Kennedy's bill also mandated to control private industry making private citizens subject to this law as well. To the naïve, this might sound like a good thing, but is far from being good. As Jefferson said, "The legitimate powers of government reach actions only, & not opinions." The most ludicrous thing a people could do would be to allow the government to become the moral authority over them. Why would you ever allow immoral men dictate your morals? Our founding fathers understood this and did not give any power to the government to make such laws. As a matter of fact, the Constitution was written to prevent such laws as my earlier articles show.

The moral conscience of the people does not need to come from a government law that threatens to arrest, imprison, or fine them or deny privileges or work as this civil rights act does. We do not need threats and intimidation. What we needed was a leader from among the people to help bring about awareness and social reform through education and enlightenment so the people could make an informed transition by their own free will. This is exactly what the civil rights activist Reverend Martin Luther King Jr. was doing when this bill was drafted.

Martin Luther King Jr. despised racism and segregation and believed that all men should regard each other as equals and hold each other in equal respect as our Creator intended. He believed that all Americans should come together as one united community to abolish racism. Do you notice how his beliefs and those of our founding fathers when they penned, "We hold these truths to be self-evident, that all men are created equal, that they are endowed by their Creator with certain unalienable Rights, that among these are Life, Liberty and the pursuit of Happiness," in the Declaration of Independence are identical?

Did you know that the first name of Martin Luther King Sr. and Jr. was originally Michael? Both changed their first names to honor a white German minister who preached Christian revival. These two men practiced what they preached especially when it came to disregarding the race of an individual.

Martin Luther King Jr. held peaceful demonstrations and marches preaching equality for all and unity, and he was effective at that. He was actually bringing an awareness of the social injustices of segregation and racism, and there was a definite change in the national conscience when it came to the races. When Martin Luther King Jr. started his marches in the 1950s, they contained mostly blacks, but by the mid to late 1960s, his marches consisted of whites, blacks, Hispanics, Catholics, Christians, Jews, etc. He was having a major impact on the moral conscience of America. And this change of conscience came by the people's own free will, not through coercion and threats. This was a problem for the Marxists and our government as Martin Luther King Jr.'s reformation was based on the principles of Christianity and the Word of God and was bringing a national awareness of the gospel as well as the social injustice going on.

As the intent of the Marxists is to eliminate Christianity, Martin Luther King Jr. became a threat that needed to be eliminated. Once he was eliminated, the government could step back in as the messiah of the people, and the way they did that was to add special protected classes to the Civil Rights Act of 1964.

On the exterior, having special protected classes seems harmless, even beneficial, but let's look at the subconscious effect that has. The special protected classes become the class of emancipation, and of course, the class that is not singled out as protected becomes the class of oppression as taught by Marx. And who is portrayed as the class of oppression? White Christian males. Think about it. If the only way you could obtain equality for the class of emancipation was through a law, there must be a genuine, natural supremacy of the class of oppression. That means that there is a genuine natural inferiority of the class of emancipation. Why else for the need of the law?

With the Civil Rights Act, the white Christian male does not need protection because he is secure in his being while the rest of the culture requires this protection to gain equality. And there is definitely a hierarchy to this perceived inferiority. This hierarchy is based on our teachings of evolution. All good Marxists believe that the darker the person, the less evolved and more inferior that person is. This is why so many white liberals hold the belief that the white man needs to help the dark man. Who needs help? The person with lesser ability. Whom do we look to for help? A person with superior ability and skill. Why would you look to a person with equal or lesser abilities for help? And why would you expect to receive a hand up if you did not feel inferior?

The result of all this is the dependency of the class of emancipation on the government so it can achieve equality with the class of oppression. The government gains control over the people, and the people become the slaves of the government dependent on their master. We see the effects of this subliminal manipulation throughout our society today. Let me give you a couple of examples, but first let me explain one thing. For Marxism to flourish, it needs to seize and maintain three disciplines: politics, to create the laws to control the people; education, to indoctrinate the people to their way of thinking; and the media, propagandists, so they can control what the people think.

Have you noticed how the media emphasizes that when a black male becomes successful, he is paired with a white woman, the prize? Why are not black woman the prize? The class of emancipation elevates itself to the level of the class of oppression. A good satire of this is a movie called *White Chicks* that depicts all white women as simpleminded tramps and successful black athletes as people who want to be with only white chicks.

Recently, a group of white boys from a Catholic high school were at a rally where there were some black protesters and a Native American protester. One of the boys had a MAGA (Make America Great Again) hat on. The media bombarded the airways with images of the Native American pounding a drum in the face of the white boy claiming that the white boy had gotten into the Indian's face and was smirking at him. The media also claimed that the white boys were discriminating against the black protestors. However, video of the actual incident went viral on social media, and it proved that the racial bigots were the black protesters and the native American protester, and they were discriminating against the white Christian boys. The media was forced to make a weak apology, and they quickly brushed the story under the rug. The story was intended to cause a rift between the class of emancipation and the class of oppression, but the story backfired, and it gave the American people a clear picture of what the media is doing.

This is far from the only story where the media deliberately caused a rift between whites and (what is the politically correct term?) minorities. Have you noticed that every time a white police officer or white person harms a black man or woman, the press emphasizes the race of each party and the story is rebroadcast a hundred times condemning the racial injustice? But if a black officer harms a black man or even a white man, no mention of race is mentioned. We see story after story of black males assaulting whites and other races, but never does the press emphasize that fact. Come on, people, think about it. This is a deliberate act of mind control, and good slaves fall for it every time.

Marxists pit not only races but also genders against each other. A prime example of this was Hillary Clinton's campaign for the presidency. Her past performance proved that she was incompetent for the job. She had proven herself a failure time and time again with Benghazi being her greatest failure resulting in the needless murders of American ambassadors. Yet the party wanted her in as she was a good Marxist soldier. So the politburo, I mean the press, cleaned her up, and she ran a campaign based on the empowerment of women, the class of emancipation rising up to overthrow the evil class of oppression. Remember her rally call, equal pay for equal work for women? The Equal Pay Act making it mandatory for women to receive equal pay was enacted in 1963 by a white Catholic male by the name of John F. Kennedy. It was already the law of the land. If she had won, what would she have done? Point to the law and take credit for Kennedy's achievement? Hillary Clinton played women for fools. She created a dilemma that did not exist. The sad fact is that so many women played the role.

So what do we, white Christian males, the class of oppression, actually think? We are the ones who penned, "All men are created equal, that they are endowed by their Creator with certain unalienable Rights" in the Declaration of Independence, and we believe what God had Moses write when he wrote, "So God created man in His own image, in the image of God He created him; male and female He created them" (Genesis 1:27 NIV). Do you ever wonder what this nation would look like if the class of emancipation believed this too?

The American people have been subdued by some masterful psychological casuistry causing them to acquiesce to slavery. Many of you have viewed these lessons and are still content with the way things are. Many of you have an innate predisposition to slavery. You are content having someone telling you what to do, what to think, and how to act. You make excellent Marxist soldiers.

However, many more of us who have an innate predisposition to independence and freedom don't need people telling us how to think or live. We live by that creed I read in my opening chapter. Those of us who cherish our freedom understand that we need to recover what's been stolen from us.

Do you need more proof that our government wants nothing less than our enslavement? Let's go back to the new Real ID card the government is forcing us to have. Without it, you soon won't be able to go into your bank; the reason is because they are federally insured, so the government is taking control of the banks, and with that, they control the people. Control someone's cash flow and you control or own them.

But the card will not be enough for them. Soon, they will brand people by making them accept a microchip in their skin if they want to buy or sell anything. Once branded, the government will own them like a rancher owns a cow. Remember, this Real ID is illegal as it violates Article 4, Section 1; Article 1, Section 8, Paragraph 18; and the Tenth Amendment.

I know this sounds like some radical thinking, but please give it a lot of thought before you dismiss it. If what you see going on in our society today matches what I am saying, I must be right.

I will continue this discussion in article 14. Know there is hope.
—April 30, 2015

Article 13: Subterfuge and Solution Part 2

So is there a solution for this tyrannical, rogue government? Fortunately, yes there is. First, people will have to realize that there is a problem and what that problem is. Then we need to get the state governments to step up to the plate and exert the authority they have. As I have stated throughout my previous articles, the Constitution gives the states all the power needed to admonish the federal government and correct constitutional abuses; it is mandated by the Constitution that they do so (Article 6, Paragraphs 2–3). Then we need to have a convention of the states to draft and ratify two amendments that address and correct the problems with our federal government that I have drawn attention to with these articles. A group, the Convention of States, is calling for such amendments, and one of the proposed amendments by them has to do with making it mandatory that the federal government obey the Tenth Amendment.

Why does our federal government, all three branches, believe it can ignore the Tenth Amendment of the Constitution? It's time for a history lesson. In 1819, just sixteen years after Chief Justice John Marshall established the right of the Supreme Court to conduct judicial review of federal laws, he presided in the case *McCulloch v. Maryland*. Some background: Congress had passed a law that allowed it to operate federal banks, but Maryland stated that that was a violation of Amendment 10. Here are excerpts from Marshall's opinion.

> The first question made in the cause is, has Congress power to incorporate a bank? ... The power now contested was exercised by the first Congress elected under the present Constitution. ... The original act was permitted to expire; but a short experience of the embarrassments to which the refusal to revive it exposed the government convinced those who were most prejudiced against the measure of its necessity, and induced the passage of the present law. ... This government is acknowledged by all to be one of enumerated powers. / The principle, that it can exercise only the powers granted to it [is] now universally admitted. **But the question respecting the extent of the powers actually granted, is perpetually arising, and will probably continue to arise, as long as our system shall exist ...** Among the enumerated powers, we do not find

that of establishing a bank or creating a corporation. But there is no phrase in the instrument which, ... requires that everything granted shall be expressly and minutely descried. **Even the 10th amendment, which was framed for the purpose of quieting the excessive jealousies which had been excited, omits the word "expressly," and declares only that "The powers not delegated to the United States, nor prohibited to the States, are reserved to the States or to the People."** ; / thus leaving the question, whether the particular power which may become the subject of contest has been delegated to the one government, or prohibited to the other, to depend on a fair construction of the whole instrument. ... Almost all compositions contain words which, taken in their rigorous sense would convey a meaning different from that which is obviously intended ...

Okay, you get a pretty clear picture of what's going on with this opinion. What we have here is a classic case study in corruption. Here is the man who sixteen years earlier gave us the best description of what a constitution was, what it meant for a law to be unconstitutional, and what restraining nature a constitution has. But in this opinion, he marginalized the Constitution and minced words. He was playing less the part of an unbiased judge and was playing politics. Notice how in one breath he stated that it was universally accepted that the powers granted were enumerated, but in the next breath, he questioned what the extent of those powers were. All you have to do is read Section 8 of Article 1. Like any good politician, he was lying to make his case.

Let me point out the two obvious lies. First, he tried to justify his decision by claiming that the Tenth Amendment did not use the word *expressly*; no, it used a different word conveying the same message. The word used was reserved. Have you ever reserved a table at a restaurant and expected to be seated with strangers? You reserved it with the intent of having it for your party alone. When something is reserved, it is expressly for the person or entity it was reserved for. So Marshall lied about the extent of the restriction being placed by the Tenth Amendment. Also, there are three other locations in the instrument, the Constitution, that make it clear that all legislation by the federal government must be derived expressly from the Constitution (Article 1, Section 8, Paragraph 18; Article 3, Section 2, Paragraph 1; and Article 6, paragraph 2).

The second obvious lie is the reason he gave for the making of the Tenth Amendment. He stated it was out of excessive jealousies; however, the preamble to the Bill of Rights as it is still called today clearly says this.

> THE Conventions of a number of the States, having at the time of their adopting the Constitution, expressed a desire, in order to prevent misconstruction or abuse of its powers, that further declaratory and restrictive clauses should be added.

It was not out of jealousy that the founders wrote the Tenth Amendment; it was a means of clarification and an attempt to avert the federal government's abuse of its power, the very thing Justice Marshall was doing in his opinion.

It is obvious that Marshall was in favor of the law and wanted it to remain, but he had no idea how the First Congress derived the power to make the first law or where the present Congress derived the power either. Marshall was a linear thinker who could not think outside his box. Never in his opinion did he cite the location in the Constitution from which Congress could have derived the power to operate a bank. Had he cited that Article 1, Section 8 Paragraph 18 gave them the authority to make necessary and proper departments to support the rest of Section 8 and that Section 8 Paragraph 5 gave them the authority "to coin money and regulate the value thereof," he would have made his case.

A federally run bank would be an easy and logical place for the federal government to distribute the gold and silver coins it minted and regulate the value of the money through interest loans. Unlike the Federal Reserve Bank we have today, which is unconstitutional as it is not run by the government but by a private entity, these banks would be constitutional as they would be maintained by the government and the Constitution gives the legislature the power to establish agencies to carry out the work of the federal government. Ultimately, he made the right decision but for all the wrong reasons. For decades, Congress has been using his reasoning to usurp the states' authority.

This case shows us three other things. First, lifetime appointments lead to corrupt judges. Second, we need better accountability over our judges. Third, it makes it clear why our founding fathers outlawed case law in this country.

So this case is where the idea that the federal government did not have to adhere to the Tenth Amendment originated. Remember, no law can be passed by Congress, no president can nullify any part of the Constitution via executive order, and no judge can nullify any portion of the Constitution. The Tenth Amendment is as much of the Constitution as any other part they are required to obey, and it is not up to the federal government to enforce it. Enforcing the Tenth Amendment is the responsibility of state governments, and it is the responsibility of the federal government to obey it. An amendment designed to force the federal government to obey the Tenth Amendment would probably be ignored by the federal government as well. We need amendments that address the problems I have outlined in these articles.

I have drafted two proposed amendments that would bring this country back to being a free nation again and forever correct the problems that allowed our federal government to run amuck in the first place, and a third amendment that addresses our immigration problem. Here are my three amendments.

Amendment Twenty-Eight

Section 1. No inferior court of the federal government shall have the power to declare any Act, Law, Tax, or Duty unconstitutional. In any Case that a judge of an inferior court should deem the matter at hand to be in opposition to the Constitution of the United States, they shall appeal the case before the Supreme Court. All courts within the United States of America shall be Courts of Justice and not courts of law.

In accordance with Section 1 of Article 3 of the Constitution of the United States, inferior court Judges shall hold their offices during good Behavior. In addition to impeachment for criminal activity as required in Article 2, Section 4, Bad Behavior by which a Judge shall be removed and or imprisoned Shall consist of, but not limited to; Hearing a case outside their venue and Jurisdiction, dictating new laws, (case law) which is in violation of Article 1, Section 1 of this Constitution, attempting to extend their authority beyond the courtroom, attempting to enforce judgments not supported by laws derived by the proper legislative body, attempting to overturn any law voted on by the majority of the people or laws of the several States, and consistently making poor decisions or a decision that is an offense to this nation's heritage or is contradictive to this Constitution. The Historical reasons for impeachments shall be considered as well when determining what bad behavior is.

The Supreme Court shall convene once a year for nine weeks starting the second week in January and adjourn at the end of the first week in March. All Supreme Court Justices shall be appointed for one term of six years. The total number of Supreme Court Judges sitting on the bench shall not exceed seven. [Sources for nominees for the position of United States Supreme Court Justice will be any officer of the armed forces who has reached the rank of O-4, or any enlisted member of the armed forces who has reached the rank of E-7, and any law enforcement officer, State or federal, who has served honorably for at least 12 years.]

The President of the United States shall have the authority to remove any judge of an inferior court, in violation of the aforementioned reasons, from his office without the consent of Congress. The House of Representatives must consent by a majority vote in the case of removal of a Supreme Court justice for an impeachment. The Senate shall try the case. In Addition, the Executive of the State in which an offending judge presides, and/or the People of that State by a majority vote, may remove an inferior court Judge of the United States or judge of the several States, for the afore mentioned reasons.

Section 2. The first paragraph of the 17th Amendment to the Constitution of the United States is hereby repealed, and Section 3 of Article 1 of the Constitution of the United States is reinstated.

Senators shall be entitled to but one term of office, and a Representative of the House of Representatives shall be entitled to three terms of office if so elected by the People of their respective State. Each State in the Union shall be entitled to three Representatives and only three.

Congress shall be convened once every two years starting on the second Tuesday in January and adjourning no later than the first Thursday in April. They may adjourn earlier with the consensus of both houses and the President. Elections for Congress shall be on the odd number years and the sessions will be held on the even number years.

No Bill presented by Congress or Law enacted shall exceed ten pages in length, and all bills presented in either house of Congress shall be voted on in a timely manner, and the act of filibuster shall be illegal. No clause within the Constitution of the United States designed to protect the rights of the States and/or the People may be repealed.

Section 3. In Accordance with Article VI of this Constitution, All aspects of the Constitution of the United States shall be strictly adhered to, and in addition to Impeachment as prescribed in Article 2, Section 4 of this Constitution, any civil officer of the United States to include judicial Officers both of the Supreme and inferior courts, Senators and Representatives, the President and Vice President, and the Members of the several State Legislatures, and all executive and judicial offices of the several States who are found in violation of this Constitution shall be Indicted, tried, judged, and punished, subject to imprisonment of up to ten years and fined up to $50,000.00.

Any and all Laws, Offices, or Agencies, past, present, or future, formed outside the confines and in violation of the Constitution of the United States, are null and void.

The Supreme Court, the Supreme Courts of the Several States, the President, the Executive of the several States, and a jury shall have the authority to declare an Act, Law, Tax, or Duty enacted by the Congress of United States, unconstitutional, and the people shall retain the right to petition these entities directly for redness of constitutional grievances.

Section 4. The President and Vice President shall be entitled to one term of six years.

Section 5. This Amendment shall, in accordance with Article V of the Constitution of the United States, when ratified by the Legislatures of three fourths of the several States, or by Conventions in three fourths thereof, as the one or the other Mode of Ratification may be proposed by the Congress, this Amendment shall be as Part of this Constitution

My second new article would be Amendment 29.

Amendment Twenty-Nine

Section 1. In supplement to the Sixteenth Amendment. No income tax shall be laid on dividends or interest earned on a private saving account, whether it be a saving, checking or individual retirement account, and no income tax shall be collected from a gift of any size or form. No tax of any form shall be laid on an inheritance, nor shall any tax be laid on private property, real estate. Dividends on stocks and bonds are earned income.

Section 2. Income withheld shall not exceed ten percent of an earned income of which the State government shall be entitled to up to seven percent as the standard, but no less than six percent, and the United States government shall be entitled to the remaining percent except in time of open invasion and war in which the United States government shall be entitled to up to seven percent, with the standard at six percent, and the State government shall be entitled to the remaining percent, and this shall be a flat tax with no exemptions except for those whose income are below the poverty level which, at this time, is set at twenty thousand dollars per household income. No income withheld may cause a person's salary or household income to drop below poverty level.

Section 3. Congress shall have the power by law to adjust the poverty level and adjust all fines and fees in regard to the cost of living index as a result of inflation and deflation.

Section 4. This amendment is binding on the State and lesser governments as it is the United States Government. This amendment is a privilege and immunity for the citizens of the United States, and of the several States.

This amendment is to protect us directly. Controlling the amount the government can earn will control what it does. This is important.

This next amendment is designed to end abuse of our immigration laws by certain foreign nationalists by circumventing them through the birth of a child. It is also designed to save the lives of our unborn children from heartless women.

Amendment Thirty

Section 1. To be born a Citizen of the United States of America, at least one biological parent must be a Citizen of the United States of America. A newborn earns his/her citizenship upon Conception.

In Amendment 28, we take away the privilege of only one judge being able to determine whether a law passed by the legislative branch and signed by the president is unconstitutional and ensure that it is considered by more than one person. Judges are to be held to the highest standard of conduct, so we are also defining some of the types of bad behavior that would require their removal or imprisonment.

We have placed a short period of time during which the Supreme Court can hear cases. This may seem strange to you, but before Roosevelt helped make their job a full-time position so he could legislate through litigation, the justices of the Supreme Court convened for only six to nine weeks. That was it. We just put it back to the way it was meant to be. And as the vast majority of the cases they hear today are unconstitutional, once the Constitution is adhered to again, they won't have that big of a caseload anymore; nine weeks will be plenty of time.

Also, notice that term limits for their service are established. *McCulloch v. Maryland* showed that even judges can become corrupt if allowed to stay in office too long. Six years seems to be the longest the vast majority of people can stay in such a position before good intent becomes selfish gain. This is why six years is the longest any member of the three branches of government should be allowed to stay in office. Even this might be too long for some individuals.

Then we put in more watchdogs on our court system. Judges have had far too much amnesty from misconduct for far too long. We need to hold them responsible for poor judicature.

I put in brackets a clause stating that nominees for the Supreme Court should come from a military or police background; these groups are charged with enforcing the law. Lawyers on the other hand make a career of manipulating the law for the sake of their clients. It seems to me that a person trained to enforce laws would do a much better job of upholding the law as opposed to a person trained to manipulate the law. This is the only clause that could be removed and still allow for the change we desperately need.

Next, we eliminate the full-time career status of members of Congress. This way, they are no longer forced to make unnecessary laws. Then we eliminate the ability for members of Congress to introduce pork or hidden agendas in laws by requiring them to be short and to the point. Ten pages is long enough for any legitimate law.

Next, we make it obvious to all that violating the Constitution is a crime and breaking it is punishable by imprisonment.

The reason for the Twenty-Ninth Amendment is that we the people do not institute governments to burden us with excessive taxation. One of the rights of the people not enumerated but suggested in the Ninth Amendment is the right to keep what we have earned. Yes, taxes are needed, but only to a certain extent. Biblically, in 1 Samuel, 10 percent is mandated, and this is a good amount. You should be able to keep 90 percent of your earnings. Also, you should be able to build a retirement nest egg without the government's constantly sticking its hands in your pocket. This is why a flat tax is prescribed; it is fair for everyone as all pay just 10 percent. The rich whine because they claim they pay more, but the burden is the same—10 percent. I can't feel sorry for a guy making a million dollars a year who is allowed to keep $900,000 to do what he wants to with. Oh, the hardship. No. A flat tax is the fairest form of taxation.

What you have saved for your children should go to them, not some government agency and then to who knows whose pocket.

Inheritance taxes have been used to take away farms from private farmers to get them into the hands of big business for far too long. This taxation is criminal and needs to be eliminated.

Our founding fathers always equated the ownership of property with freedom, and they were right. To be truly free, we should be able to own the property we live on; it's our right. But think about this—If a government body can throw you off your property for not paying taxes, are you not merely a tenant of that property? Does not the owner of a property have the right to evict a tenant who does not pay his rent? This means no one in America is truly a free person.

Property and inheritance taxes are a form of governmental criminal behavior that needs to be eradicated. A flat tax would eliminate the government's claim for a need for such taxation. Limiting the amount of taxes the government can collect is an effective way for the people to control their government and prohibit the type of governmental abuse I've been writing about.

Article 30 prohibits foreign nationalists from coming to this country just to give birth to their children so they themselves can claim citizenship later on or take advantage of the American taxpayer by collecting privileges even we don't have. Many foreign nationalists become citizens the honest way, and allowing some to take advantage of loopholes is a slap in their and taxpayers' faces.

This amendment also ensures all of its citizens' rights are protected, even those who are not yet born.

These first two amendments address the problem we have with the federal and to a lesser degree the state governments. Anything less than these two amendments will fail to correct the governmental abuse that is so prevalent in our nation's capital. But the only way that these changes will ever happen is if we the people speak out. We need to have our voices heard. The least we can do is simply write our state representatives and let them know we want to be free, we want to take back our liberty and see that this nation is run the way our founding fathers intended. It is up to us.

—April 30, 2015

Article 14: Remedy at State Level

In Article 13, I introduced three amendments that would solve the problems we are facing with this abusive federal government. I would like to introduce a law that could be passed by state legislatures or by a referendum that would result in a dramatic curtailing of the abuses now plaguing us at the federal level of government.

Nevada law on Constitutional Obedience

1. In accordance with Article 6 Paragraph 3, and Article 4, Section 4 of the United States Constitution, and in accordance with Article 4 Section 18, Subsection 1 of the State of Nevada Constitution, the State of Nevada's (New Mexico, Utah, etc.) Legislative branch, the Executive branch and the State Judicial branch, have the legal authority and obligation to review all laws passed by the United States Congress, and all rulings of the United States Judicial Branch to include Supreme Court rulings, and any such Act, statute, or ruling that is found to be repugnant of the United States Constitution is to be declared void and disregarded. Any Agency created by the United States Congress that is declared by the State of Nevada to be in violation of the United States Constitution shall be powerless to act within the State of Nevada.

2. In addition the State of Nevada has the legal authority and obligation to assume any and all powers vested to it by the United States Constitution in Article 4 Sections 1 through 4 and the 10th Amendment, that are being usurped by the government of the United States.

3. And in accordance with Article 1 Section 1 of the United States Constitution, neither the president nor the U.S. Judicial Branch are given the power to legislate, and as such the State of Nevada is obligated to disregard any law or executive order by the president of the United States, and any case law rendered by any member of the U.S. Judicial Branch to include the United States Supreme Court.

4. In addition to this, as no authority is granted to the United States Judicial branch to conduct a judicial review of State laws, the State of Nevada is legally obligated to disregard any such renderings.

5. As the United States Constitution is the Supreme Law of the Land, and as such it is a crime to violate the Constitution, the State of Nevada has the legal authority and obligation to indict, try, judge and punish any person sworn by oath to support the Constitution, to include the president of the United States, any member of the United States congress, any member of the United States Judicial branch including the members of the US Supreme Court, and all federal agents who violate any portion of the United States Constitution within their borders, or makes a law or ruling from within the Nation's Capital with the intent to subjugate the State of Nevada or any of its citizenry to an unconstitutional act. Whereas any member of the federal government that is violating the United States Constitution is acting outside the authority of the Constitution, and as such, they are acting as private citizens and are not protected by Article 3 Section 2 Clause 4, (to controversies to which the United States shall be

a party;) of the United States Constitution, and are subject to this law.

6. The State of Nevada shall have the authority to issue an arrest warrant to any person who is in violation of this law within the State of Nevada, and on any property owned by the United States, as we are a member, to include the Nation's Capital, and transport them to appear before the State Supreme Court, whom shall have original authority over all such cases, so they may be subject to Indictment, charged with Constitutional Disobedience, Trial, Judgment, and Punishment. Upon Conviction the suspect, if a member of U.S. Congress, or the President, or any member of the U.S. Judicial branch, shall be sentence to up to 10 years in prison, and fined no more than $50,000.00. An agent of the federal government in violation of this law, when convicted shall be sentenced to up to 3 years in prison, and fined no more than $2,000.00.

7. This law is not in substitute of Impeachment as prescribed in Article 2 Section 4 of the U.S. Constitution, and any member of the U.S. Congress, the president, any member of the U.S. Judicial branch, shall be impeached and convicted as a result of conviction of this Statute. Any member of the U.S. House of Representatives for the State of Nevada that fells to impeach any member of the U.S Congress, the president, or vice president, or a U.S. Judge for treason, bribery, or High crime, and misdemeanors; and any member of the U.S. Senate that represents the State of Nevada that fells to convict the afore mentioned parties, will be in

violation of Article 2 Section 4 and subject to the full force of this law.

8. In accordance with and in obedience to Article 6 Sections 2 (The Constitution shall be the supreme law of the land) and 3, no State congressman shall propose any bill or enact any law that is repugnant to the U.S. Constitution, or the Constitution of the State of Nevada. Nor will the legislators of the county or municipalities make or enforce any ordinances that are repugnant to the U.S. Constitution or State Constitution. Nor will the Governor of the State of Nevada sign into law or enforce any law by the State legislature; nor will any County councilman or city mayor enforce any ordinance made by the local legislatures, that is repugnant to the U.S. Constitution, and/or State Constitution. Every judge within the State shall strictly adhere to Article 6 Section 2 of the U.S. Constitution. Any violation of this statue by the afore mentioned State and Local officials will result in Indictment, charged with Constitutional Disobedience, Trial, Judgment, and Punishment, and upon conviction shall be sentenced to up to 3 years in prison, and fined no more than $10,000.00.

9. In addition, any agent of the State, County, or Municipal government who attempts to enforce a law, whether it be a federal, State, county, or municipal law, that is repugnant to the U.S. Constitution or the State Constitution, shall be in violation of this statue and subject to indictment, trial, judgment, and punishment, and upon conviction be sentenced up to 1 year in prison and fined no more $1,000.00.

10. The Statute of limitations for this law shall be 10 years.

Did you notice that I started this law with what I call a patence of nobility? I believe that every law at every level of government should start out identifying precisely where the law is deriving its authority to be made. If lawmakers are forced to start off a law in this way, I believe there would be fewer abuses of the law of our land.

Notice also that I continued to identify where in the Constitution I derived the power to enforce various clauses. In this way, no activist judge can declare the law unconstitutional just because it offends him. Judges are not supposed to play politics. Their job is to uphold the laws made by the proper legislature. For a judge to practice politics from the bench is bad behavior and would subject that judge to impeachment and under this law imprisonment as well.

As you see, this law is constitutional and can be adopted by every state. But we the people need to speak up and demand that our state legislatures start representing us in a manner worthy of a free people. People, it's time for us to grow a backbone and stand up for ourselves. Nothing will change if we leave our fate in the hands of the politicians; it'll only get worse. If you're in a state that gives the people the right to propose referendums, take charge and put your state's constitutional authority where Nevada's lawmaking authority is derived from, and make this law your own. If you're in state in which only legislators can introduce a law, get on your legislators. Hand this law to one of them and say, "Get on it." Ultimately, our freedom relies on us.

—July 27, 2017

This ends my articles and video scripts. I hope you found them insightful and enlightening. The amendments I proposed and the new state law I drafted will be enough to start this nation back on the road to sanity. I hope that after this book is published, the true rulers of this nation, we the people, will demand change. Many are anxious for change. I have read social media posts and heard many people I consider to be level headed talk of civil war. That kind of talk makes me nervous for various reasons, and I feel it necessary to discuss the legality and efficaciousness of such an endeavor. But before I do that, I would like to look at viable options to bring about the kind of change this nation so desperately needs to bring us back to being a free constitutional republic.

The easiest and most effective way would be for President Trump to gain a thorough understanding of the Constitution and do his constitutional duty to enforce it. He must understand that what Congress and the Supreme Court and the lesser courts are doing is in deliberate contrast to what they are permitted to do in every aspect of what they are currently doing; it is nothing less than rebellion against the law of the land, our Constitution.

Let me give you some examples of what I am talking about, and look at some recent laws that have been passed. HB 4334 Dignity in Aging Act 2019 makes special provisions in the care of the elderly. Although this sounds wonderful only the states, under Article 4 section 1, have the authority for public acts. Therefore this act is a usurpation of the states right and is rebellion against the Constitution.

HB 263 To Rename the Oyster Bay National Wildlife Refuge as the Congressman Lester Wolff Oyster Bay National Wildlife Refuge Act. Although this act is dedicated to renaming a national wildlife refuge supposedly of federal property, where in the Constitution gives the federal government the authority to maintain wildlife refuges? Again this act usurps the states authority by violating; Article 1 Section 8 Paragraph 17, Article 4, Section 1 and 4, and the Tenth Amendment, and is therefore rebellion against the Constitution.

SB 1822 Broadband DATA Act 2020 requires the FCC to set up a data set of geo-coded information for all broadband service locations; broadband maps. FCC must provide data collection and submission assistance to Indian tribes; small service providers; consumers; and state, local, and tribal governments. This act scares me. Why does the government need to keep track of this information? What is the ultimate use for this information? There is no provision in the Constitution that allows congress to make laws regulating communications, so they are violating the Tenth Amendment, and again usurping the states authority. What these House of Representatives and Senators did were deliberate acts of rebellion. By law, the president has to charge them with.

Title 18 USC ss 2383 Rebellion or Insurrection

Whoever incites, sets on foot, assists or engages in any rebellion or insurrection against the **Authority of the United States, or the laws thereof**, or gives aid or comfort thereof, shall be fined under this title or imprisoned not more than ten years or both, and shall be incapable of holding any office under the United States. (The Authority of the United States is the Constitution.) and,

Title 18 USC 371 Conspiracy

If two or more persons conspire either to commit any offense against the United States, or to defraud the United States, or any agency thereof in any manner, or for any purpose, and one or more of such persons do any act to effect the object of the conspiracy, each shall be fined under this title or imprisoned not more than 5 years or both.

Our civil servants are to be held to the highest level of ethical behavior, not the lowest, and they can and must be charged with felony crimes when they commit them. Remember what you read in my articles; they are exempt only from petty offenses, not crimes. Rebellion and insurrection against the Constitution are definitely felonies.

The Constitution allows Congress's oversight of only their respective houses, not of the federal government or the president except as it concerns the approvals by the Senate on treaties and choices of appointees of heads of state. Beyond this, Congress is in violation of Article 2, Section 1, Paragraph 1 of the Constitution, and this too is rebellion.

Our federal courts are in rebellion every time they declare case law as this is in violation of Article 1, Section 1 of the Constitution and any time they hear a case that is the states' Eleventh Amendment rights.

Members of Congress, ex-presidents, and federal judges should and have to be indicted, tried, convicted, and punished under title 18 USC 2383 Rebellion and Insurrection and Title 18 USC 371 Conspiracy. By law, the president can do no less.

Another action that can be taken to correct the current despotism we have in our federal and state governments is by the officers of our militia, the army and air national guards, and the navy and army. Read these excerpts from articles by Alexander Hamilton in Federalist Papers 26, 27, 28, 29.

FEDERALIST PAPER 26

> The provision for the support of a military force will always be a favorable topic for declamation. As often as the question comes forward, the public attention will be roused and attracted to the subject, by the party in opposition; and if the majority should be really disposed to **exceed the proper limits**, the community will be warned of the danger, and will have an opportunity of taking measures to guard against it. Independent of parties in the national legislature itself, as often as the period of discussion arrived, the State legislatures, who will always be not

only vigilant but suspicious and jealous guardians of the rights of the citizens against encroachments from the federal government, will constantly have their attention awake to the conduct of the national rulers, and will be ready enough, if anything improper appears, to sound the alarm to the people, and not only to be the **voice**, but, if necessary, the **arm** of their discontent.

Schemes to subvert the liberties of a great community require time to mature them for execution. An army, so large as seriously to menace those liberties, could only be formed by progressive augmentations; which would suppose, not merely a temporary combination between the legislature and executive, but a continued conspiracy for a series of time. Is it probable that such a combination would exist at all? Is it probable that it would be persevered in, and transmitted along through all the successive variations in a representative body, which biennial elections would naturally produce in both houses? Is it presumable, that every man, the instant he took his seat in the national Senate or House of Representatives, would commence a traitor to his constituents and to his country? Can it be supposed that there would not be found one man, discerning enough to detect so atrocious a conspiracy, or bold or honest enough to apprise his constituents of their danger? If such presumptions can fairly be made, there ought at once to be an end of all delegated authority. The people should resolve to recall all the powers they have heretofore parted with out of their own hands, and to divide themselves into as many States as there are counties, in order that they may be able to manage their own concerns in person.

If such suppositions could even be reasonably made, still the concealment of the design, for any duration, would be impracticable. It would be announced, by the very circumstance of augmenting the army to so great an extent in time of profound peace. What colorable reason could be assigned, in a country so situated, for such vast augmentations of the military force? It is impossible that the people could be long deceived; and **the destruction** of the project, **and of the projectors**, would quickly follow the discovery.

FEDERALIST PAPER 27

A turbulent faction in a State may easily suppose itself able to contend with the friends to the government in that State; but it can hardly be so infatuated as to imagine itself a match for the combined efforts of the Union. If this reflection be just, there is less danger of resistance from irregular combinations of individuals to the authority of the Confederacy than to that of a single member ... Man is very much a creature of habit. A thing that rarely strikes his senses will generally have but little influence upon his mind. A government continually at a distance and out of sight can hardly be expected to interest the sensations of the people. The inference is, that the authority of the Union, and the affections of the citizens towards it, will be strengthened, rather than weakened, by its extension to what are called matters of internal concern; and will have less occasion to recur to force, in proportion to the familiarity and comprehensiveness of its agency. The more it circulates through those channels and currents in which the passions of mankind naturally flow, the less will it require the aid of the violent and perilous expedients of compulsion … It merits particular attention in this place, that the laws of the Confederacy, as to the **enumerated** and **legitimate** objects of its jurisdiction, will become the **supreme law** of the land; to the observance of which all officers, legislative, executive, and judicial, in each State, will be bound by the sanctity of an oath. Thus the legislatures, courts, and magistrates, of the respective members, will be incorporated into the operations of the national government **as far as its just and constitutional authority extends**; and will be rendered auxiliary to the enforcement of its laws.

FEDERALIST PAPER 28

If the representatives of the people betray their constituents, there is then no resource left but in the exertion of that **original right of self-defense which is paramount to all positive forms of government**, and which against the **usurpations** of the national rulers, may be exerted with infinitely better prospect of success than against those of the rulers of an individual state. **In a single state, if the persons entrusted with supreme power become usurpers**, the different parcels, subdivisions, or districts of which it consists, having no distinct government in each, can take no regular measures for defense. **The citizens must rush tumultuously to arms, without concert, without system, without resource; except in their courage and despair.** The usurpers, clothed with the forms of legal authority, can too often crush the opposition in embryo ...

In this situation there must be a peculiar coincidence of circumstances to insure success to the popular resistance ... The obstacles to usurpation and the facilities of resistance increase with the increased extent of the state, **provided the citizens understand their rights and are disposed to defend them.** The natural strength of the people in a large community, in proportion to the artificial strength of the government, is greater than in a small, and of course more competent to a struggle with the attempts of the **government to establish a tyranny. But in a confederacy the people, without exaggeration, may be said to be entirely the masters of their own fate.** Power being almost always the rival of power, the general government will at all times stand ready to check the usurpations of the state governments, and these will have the same disposition towards the general government. The people, by throwing themselves into either scale, will infallibly make it preponderate. If their rights are invaded by either, they can make use of the other as the instrument of redress. How wise will it be in them by cherishing the union to preserve to themselves an advantage which can never be too highly prized!. ... If the federal army should be able to quell the resistance of one State, the distant States would have it in their power to make head with fresh forces. The advantages obtained in one place must be abandoned to subdue the opposition in others; and the moment the part which had been reduced to submission was left to itself, its efforts would be renewed, and its resistance revive.

FEDERALIST PAPER 29

Where in the name of common-sense, are our fears to end if we may not trust our sons, our brothers, our neighbors, our fellow-citizens? What shadow of danger can there be from men who are daily mingling with the rest of their countrymen and who participate with them in the same feelings, sentiments, habits and interests? What reasonable cause of apprehension can be inferred from a power in the Union to prescribe regulations for the militia, and to command its services when necessary, while the particular States are to have the **sole and exclusive appointment of the officers?** If it were possible seriously to indulge a jealousy of the militia upon any conceivable establishment under the federal government, **the circumstance of the officers being in the appointment of the States ought at once to extinguish it**."

Hamilton was arguing in these articles for the necessity of a limited and small standing army and the need of a well-regulated state militia. He addressed the obvious concerns for protection against invading foreign forces and from domestic civil unrest, and he addressed the need for military intervention from governmental usurpation. It is obvious in his writings that he did not consider that a plausible threat as he believed that the structure of the Constitution had sufficient safeguards to prevent ever so vile an undertaking, but still, he gave credence to the use of military force to quell a rogue government.

I believe that Hamilton and the other founding fathers would be disheartened and dismayed that what they believed could never happen in this country—a tyrannical government—is now the accepted norm. Hamilton and his colleagues never thought that a plutocracy would emerge from the shadows and have the wealth, patience, and depravity to subvert the legitimate government with a Marxist form of government more conducive to their goals. Read *The deliberate dumbing down of America* by Charlotte Isabite and David Rockefeller's book *David Rockefeller: Memoirs* to understand what I am talking about. A conspiracy is not a theory when there are confessions.

Notice how he relies on the fact that as the militia comprises "our sons, our brothers, our neighbors, our fellow-citizens," they would take appropriate action if it became known that government officials would betray our trust and usurp the legitimate power of the people subjugating us to a form of rule never intended. In short, a legitimate role of the militia is to guard us from the criminal actions of our federal and state representatives.

But I would like to make this argument. Do not the members of the US Army and Navy consist of "our sons, our brothers, our neighbors, our fellow-citizens"? As a veteran of the US Air Force, I can assure you that we are required to take an oath to support the Constitution, follow the lawful orders of the commander in chief, and protect this nation from threats both domestic and abroad. The true authority of this nation is not the president or Congress and definitely not the Supreme Court or lesser courts. It is the Constitution itself. Does this not mean that the ultimate goal of the US military is the same in this case as is the militias' specifically to extinguish a rogue government? I assert it is. How can the members of the military fulfill their oaths to support the Constitution and still comply with unconstitutional and thus unlawful orders? How can they stand behind civil servants who are rebelling against that document? If the officers of the US military and the states' militias are to act honorably, it is their duty to remove the present form of government and reestablish the constitutional form of government we are meant to be. I have little hope of this ever happening as recent history shows that if officers of the armed forces act in an honorable fashion, they are either ostracized or court-martialed, and I doubt they have the courage to band together and do the right thing.

This leaves the people and my original topic of the legitimacy of civil war. As we can see in the passages that we just read from the Federalist Papers, Hamilton and the rest of the founding father were convinced of the morality and necessity of the people to forcibly replace criminal conspirators usurping government authority. Would that be in concert with the Constitution a lawful act? Emphatically yes.

One reason the federal government has to call forth the militia is to suppress insurrections (Article 1, Section 8, Paragraph 15), and to the casual observer, this is what this action would appear to be. However, the casual observer would be wrong. Insurrection is when a faction strives to overthrow the legitimate government. As I have proven throughout this book, civil servants usurping the delegated authority that we the people handed them have abandoned the Constitution and are nothing more than criminals. The rise of the people will not be for the overthrow of the government but for the expelling of the old guards so that new guards can once again liberate us. This war would then be more a resolution rather than a revolution. The action of the people would be a posse comitatus rather than an insurrection.

As I stated earlier in this book, the Constitution is an extension of the Declaration of Independence, and both are equally the law of the land. The Declaration was the first law to delineate and protect certain God-given rights. Let us look at this law and these rights.

> We hold these truths to be self-evident, that all men
> are created equal, that they are endowed by their

> Creator with certain unalienable Rights, that among these are Life, Liberty and the pursuit of Happiness.--That to secure these rights, Governments are instituted among Men, deriving their just powers from the consent of the governed, --That whenever any Form of Government becomes destructive of these ends, it is the Right of the People to **alter** or to abolish it ...

> But when a long train of abuses and usurpations, pursuing invariably the same Object evinces a design to reduce them under absolute Despotism, **it is their right, it is their duty**, to throw off such Government, and **to provide new Guards** for their future security.

As you can see, not only would this resolution be a lawful act; it would also be a lawful duty for citizens to do so. But this should be our last recourse after all other avenues have been exhausted.

The biggest fear I have about this resolution is that when all the traitors have been rounded up and dealt with and the time comes to establish new guards, the patriots who executed this resolution might hesitate believing that the current Constitution is too weak to prevent a recurrence of the treachery enacted upon us. Might they be inclined to do what Hamilton suggested in Federalist Paper 26?

> The people should resolve to recall all the powers they have heretofore parted with out of their own hands, and to divide themselves into as many States as there are counties, in order that they may be able to manage their own concerns in person.

Maybe not divide quite so small as counties, but make each state its own sovereign nation or other smaller confederacies. The larger a nation becomes, the more restrictions must be placed on the government to keep it in check. The smaller a nation is, the easier it is for the people to maintain control over their elected officials.

The flaw of the present Constitution is not in its structure but in the confidence the founders placed in the people to maintain it. The founders never thought that the people could be so easily driven from their Christian heritage and adopt such an abased culture. But they had never experienced the type of propaganda devised by our media, and they never expected a plutocracy to gain control of the government, media, and education systems. As Hamilton conveyed in his writings, what has happened seems beyond approach. Because of the state of the world today, it is as imperative today as it was when the Constitution was first drafted that these states remain united states, not independent nations.

John Jay made compelling arguments in favor of a national union in Federalist Papers 2–5 that are as applicable today as they were then. I have taken the liberty to offer the patriots who might be compelled to hesitate establishing new guards under the present Constitution a more constructive alternative. I have written a new constitution that is the same in structure but has more arduous safeguards to prevent clandestine usurpation. You will notice that there are no amendments protecting our privileges and immunities. This is because they are built into the constitution. Amendments are needed only for afterthoughts. Read this constitution and you will see that it is true to the original desires of the first Constitution.

The Constitution of the United States of America
2020

We the People of the United States, Acknowledge that El Shaddai, the God of Abraham, the God of Isaac, the God of Jacob, is the one true God, and that Christ Jesus, God's only begotten Son, is the true ruler of this World and Nation, and that in

His absence, we, as His Stewarts, have the right to govern ourselves. We also acknowledge that the United States Constitution of 1789 was corrupted by unscrupulous guardians. So to this end, in Order to form a more perfect Union by placing more rigorous restraints on our governments, establish Justice, insure domestic Tranquility, provide for the common defense, promote the General welfare, and secure the truer Blessings of Liberty to ourselves and our Posterity, do ordain and establish this second Constitution for the United States of America.

Article 1

Section 1

All legislative Powers herein granted shall be vested in a Congress of the United States, which shall consist of a Senate and House of Representatives.

No power to make laws is granted to the President or judges of the United States. Executive orders, directed as law, and case law are punishable by death.

Section 2

The House of Representatives shall be composed of Members chosen every second Year (even numbered years) by the People of the several States, and a Representative of the House of Representatives shall be entitled to three terms of office if so elected by the People of their respective State. Each State in the Union shall be entitled to three Representatives and only three, and the Electors in each State shall have the Qualifications requisite for Electors of the most numerous Branch of the State Legislature.

No Person shall be a Representative who shall not have attained to the Age of twenty-five Years, and been seven Years a Citizen of the United States, and who shall not, when elected, be an Inhabitant of that State in which he shall be chosen.

When vacancies happen in the Representation from any State, the Executive Authority thereof shall issue Writs of Election to fill such Vacancies.

The House of Representatives shall choose their Speaker and other officers; and shall have the sole Power of Impeachment.

Section 3

The Senate of the United States shall be composed of two Senators from each State, chosen by the Legislature thereof for only one term of six Years; and each Senator shall have one Vote. Senators represent the State and not the people.

Immediately after they shall be assembled in Consequence of the first Election, they shall be divided as equally as may be into three Classes. The Seats of the Senators of the first Class shall be vacated at the Expiration of the second Year, of the second Class at the Expiration of the fourth Year, and of the third Class at the Expiration of the sixth Year, so that one third may be chosen every second

Year; and if Vacancies happen by Resignation, or otherwise, during the Recess of the Legislature of any State, the Executive thereof may make temporary Appointments until the next Meeting of the Legislature, which shall then fill such Vacancies. Elections shall be held every even numbered year.

No Person shall be a Senator who shall not have attained to the Age of thirty Years, and been nine Years a Citizen of the United States, and who shall not, when elected, be an Inhabitant of that State for which he shall be chosen.

The Vice President of the United States shall be President of the Senate, but shall have no Vote, unless they be equally divided.

The Senate shall choose their other officers, and also a President pro tempore, in the Absence of the Vice President, or when he shall exercise the Office of President of the United States.

The Senate shall have the sole Power to try all Impeachments. When sitting for that Purpose, they shall be on Oath or Affirmation. When the President of the United States is tried, the Chief Justice shall preside: And no Person shall be convicted without the Concurrence of two thirds of the Members present.

Judgment in Cases of Impeachment shall not extend further than to removal from Office, and disqualification to hold and enjoy any Office of honor, Trust or Profit under the United States:

but the Party convicted shall nevertheless be liable and subject to Indictment, Trial, Judgment and Punishment, according to Law.

It was not chauvinism that our forefathers did not grant the right of suffrage to Women but an extensive knowledge of history, and our American experiment of allowing women to vote has resulted in; the murder of over seventy million innocent children's lives under the pretense of a women's right of choice; a gender identity crisis, and corruption at the highest levels. For these reasons and others not mentioned, no woman shall hold an office of honor at any level of government and the right to vote shall be denied for one year for each unborn child aborted. At that time this disability may be reevaluated.

Section 4

The Times, Places and Manner of holding Elections for Senators and Representatives, shall be prescribed in each State by the Legislature thereof, as long as the elections are finalized one month prior to the assemble of Congress.

Congress shall be convened once every two years starting on the second Tuesday in January and adjourning no later than the first Thursday in April. They may adjourn earlier with the consensus of both houses and the President. Elections for Congress shall be on the even number years and the sessions will be held on the odd number years.

Section 5

Each House shall be the Judge of the Elections, Returns and Qualifications of its own Members, and a Majority of each shall constitute a Quorum to do Business; but a smaller Number may adjourn from day to day, and may be authorized to compel the Attendance of absent Members, in such Manner, and under such Penalties as each House may provide.

Each House may determine the Rules of its Proceedings, punish its Members for disorderly Behavior, and, with the Concurrence of two thirds, expel a Member.

Each House shall keep a Journal of its Proceedings, and from time to time publish the same, excepting such Parts as may in their Judgment require Secrecy; and the Yeas and Nays of the Members of either House on any question shall, at the Desire of one fifth of those Present, be entered on the Journal.

Neither House, during the Session of Congress, shall, without the Consent of the other, adjourn for more than three days, nor to any other Place than that in which the two Houses shall be sitting.

Section 6

The Senators and Representatives shall receive a Compensation for their Services, to be ascertained by Law, and paid out of the Treasury of the United States. They shall in cases of petty offence, be privileged from Arrest during their Attendance at the Session of their respective Houses, and in going to and returning from the same, but shall be held accountable for any act of Treason, Felony and Breach of the Peace; and for any Speech or Debate in either House, they shall not be questioned in any other Place.

No Senator or Representative shall, during the Time for which he was elected, be appointed to any civil Office under the Authority of the United States, which shall have been created, or the Emoluments whereof shall have been increased during such time; and no Person holding any Office under the United States, shall be a Member of either House during his Continuance in Office.

No person shall be a Senator or Representative in Congress, or elector of President and Vice-President, or hold any office, civil or military, under the United States, or under any State, who, having previously taken an oath, as a member of Congress, or as an officer of the United States, or as a member of any State legislature, or as an executive or judicial officer of any State, to support the Constitution of the United States, shall have engaged in insurrection or rebellion against the same, or given aid or comfort to the enemies thereof.

Section 7

All Bills for raising Revenue shall originate in the House of Representatives; but the Senate may propose or concur with Amendments as on other Bills.

Every Bill which shall have passed the House of Representatives and the Senate, shall, before it become a Law, be presented to the President of the United States: If he approve he shall sign it, but if not he shall return it, with his Objections to that House in which it shall have originated, who shall enter the Objections at large on their Journal, and proceed to reconsider it. If after such Reconsideration two thirds of that House shall agree to pass the Bill, it shall be sent, together with the Objections, to the other House, by which it shall likewise be reconsidered, and if approved by two thirds of that House, it shall become a Law. But in all such Cases the Votes of both Houses shall be determined by yeas and Nays, and the Names of the Persons voting for and against the Bill shall be entered on the Journal of each House respectively. If any Bill shall not be returned by the President within ten Days (Sundays excepted) after it shall have been presented to him, the Same shall be a Law, in like Manner as if he had signed it, unless the Congress by their Adjournment prevent its Return, in which Case it shall not be a Law.

Every Order, Resolution, or Vote to which the Concurrence of the Senate and House of Representatives may be necessary (except on a question of Adjournment) shall be presented to the President of the United States; and before the Same shall take Effect, shall be approved by him, or being disapproved by him, shall be re-passed by two thirds of the Senate and House of Representatives, according to the Rules and Limitations prescribed in the Case of a Bill.

No Bill presented by Congress or Law enacted shall exceed ten pages in length, and all bills presented in either house of Congress shall be voted on in a timely manner, and the act of filibuster shall be illegal. No clause within the Constitution of the United States designed to protect the rights of the States and/or the People may be repealed; No Bill of Attainder or ex post facto Law shall be passed.

Section 8

No income tax shall be laid on dividends or interest earned on a private saving account, whether it be a saving, checking or individual retirement account, and no income tax shall be collected from a gift of any size or form. No tax of any form shall be laid on an inheritance, nor shall any tax be laid on private property, real estate. The Congress shall have power to lay and collect taxes on all other forms of income, without apportionment among the several States, and without regard to any census or enumeration. Dividends on stocks and bonds are earned income.

Income withheld shall not exceed ten percent of an earned income of which the State government shall be entitled to up to seven percent as the standard, but no less than six percent, and the United States government shall be entitled to the remaining percent except in time of open invasion and war in which the United States government shall be entitled to up to seven percent, with the standard at six percent, and the State government shall be entitled to the remaining percent, and this shall be a flat tax with no exemptions except for those whose income are below the poverty level which, at this time, is set at twenty thousand dollars per household income. No income withheld may cause a person's salary or household income to drop below poverty level.

Congress shall have the power by law to adjust the poverty level and adjust all fines and fees with regards to the cost of living index as a result of inflation and deflation.

No Corporate tax shall exceed twenty percent.

The Congress shall have Power To lay and collect Taxes, Duties, Imposts and Excises, to pay the Debts and provide for the common Defense and General welfare of the United States as enumerated below; but all Duties, Imposts and Excises shall be uniform throughout the United States;

To borrow Money on the credit of the United States, but all money borrowed shall be paid back within four years;

To regulate Commerce (meaning finished merchandise, packaged, and placed on transports, and until final sell) with foreign Nations, and among the several States, and with the Indian Tribes;

To set limits on immigration, establish an uniform Rule of Naturalization, and uniform Laws on the subject of Bankruptcies throughout the United States;

To coin Money, to that purpose only gold, silver and copper may be used, regulate the Value thereof, and of foreign Coin, and fix the Standard of Weights and Measures;

To provide for the Punishment of counterfeiting the Securities and current Coin of the United States;

To establish Post Offices and post Roads and in maintaining said Roads;

To promote the Progress of Science and useful Arts, not the liberal arts, strictly By securing for limited Times to Authors and Inventors the exclusive Right to their respective Writings and Discoveries;

To develop, maintain, and regulate sources of electrical power;

To regulate air travel crossing State and International boundaries;

To regulate communication signals crossing State lines;

To constitute Tribunals inferior to the Supreme Court;

To define and punish Piracies and Felonies committed on the high Seas, and Offences against the Law of Nations;

To declare War, grant Letters of Marque and Reprisal, and make Rules concerning Captures on Land and Water;

To raise and support Armies, but no Appropriation of Money to that Use shall be for a longer Term than two Years;

To provide and maintain a Navy, Coast Guard, and an Air and Space Force;

To make Rules for the Government and Regulation of the land, air and space, and naval Forces;

To provide for calling forth the Militia to execute the Laws of the Union, suppress Insurrections and repel Invasions. A well-regulated Militia, the Army and Air National Guards, being necessary to the security of a free State, shall not be infringed, each State shall retain the ultimate control over its Militias and the President shall be a proxy;

To provide for organizing, arming, and disciplining, the Militia, and for governing such Part of them as may be employed in the Service of the United States, reserving to the States respectively, the Appointment of the Officers, and the Authority of training the Militia according to the discipline prescribed by Congress;

To exercise exclusive Legislation in all Cases whatsoever, over such District (not exceeding ten Miles square) as may, by Cession of particular States, and the Acceptance of Congress, become the Seat of the Government of the United States, and to exercise like Authority over all Places purchased by the Consent of the Legislature of the State in which the Same shall be, for the Erection of Forts, Magazines, Arsenals, dock-Yards, and other needful Buildings;--And

To make all Laws which shall be necessary and proper for carrying into Execution the foregoing powers, and all other powers Vested By this Constitution in the Government of the United States, or in any Department or Officer thereof.

Congress shall present no Bill nor pass any Act intended to enlarge or decrease the power granted in this Constitution to the Congress, President, or any Judicial Officer of the United States, and any Congressman who would proposed or indorsed a Bill or ratified such an Act shall be put to Death.

Direct taxes shall be apportioned among the several States which may be included within this Union, according to their respective Numbers, which shall be determined by a census conducted once every ten years by the several States, and the States may only inquire as to the number of persons living in a household, Citizen status of each, and ownership of residence. The Census will be conducted on the start of the decade (2020, 2030, etc.)

Section 9

To be born a Citizen of the United States of America, at least one biological parent must be a Citizen of the United States of America. A new born earned his/her citizenship upon Conception. All persons born or naturalized in the United States, and subject to the jurisdiction thereof, are citizens of the United States and of the State wherein they reside. No State, County, or Municipality, shall make or enforce any law which shall abridge the privileges or immunities of citizens of the United States; nor shall any State deprive any person of life, liberty, or property, without due process of law; nor deny to any person within its jurisdiction the equal protection of the laws.

With every right comes Duties and Obligations. Any Citizen, or person residing legally within the United States, who in public dishonors, disrespects, or condemns this nation or this nation's symbols, or who claim offense with this nation's heritage, Shall be exiled. This shall be a permanent disability.

The Privilege of the Writ of Habeas Corpus shall not be suspended, unless when in Cases of Rebellion or Invasion the public Safety may require it.

No Capitation, or other direct Tax shall be laid, unless in Proportion to the Census or enumeration herein taken by each of the several States.

No Tax or Duty shall be laid on Articles exported from any State.

No Preference shall be given by any Regulation of Commerce or Revenue to the Ports of one State over those of another; nor shall Vessels bound to, or from, one State, be obliged to enter, clear, or pay Duties in another.

No Money shall be drawn from the Treasury, but in Consequence of Appropriations made by Law; and a regular Statement and Account of the Receipts and Expenditures of all public Money shall be published at the end of their session.

No Title of Nobility shall be granted by the United States: And no Person holding any Office of Profit or Trust under them, shall, without the Consent of the Congress, accept of any present, Emolument, Office, or Title, of any kind whatever, from any King, Prince, or foreign State.

Congress shall make no law respecting an establishment of religion, specifically a one state religion, or prohibiting the free exercise thereof; that the legitimate powers of government reach actions only, and not opinions, Government shall not infringe on the affairs of the church; yet this nation is to operate on the principles of Christianity.

Congress shall make no law abridging the freedom of ethical speech;

The right of the people to be properly informed shall not be infringe in such that Congress shall make no law abridging freedom of the press. The press is obligated to report provable facts without sensationalism and without bias. Any act on the press to propagandize to influence the thoughts of the people on any subject matter is an act of treason and is punishable by death;

Congress shall make no law abridging the right of the people peaceably to assemble, and to petition the Government for a redress of grievances;

The right of the people to defend their lives, the lives of their family and loved ones, their homes and livelihoods is such that the right to keep (to retain in one's power or possession, to have in custody for security or preservation) and bear, (worn either openly or concealed), Arms, (any weapon one is comfortable and proficient with in defending themselves, or in a time of need this country), shall not be infringed. In addition to security and defense, arms are for lawful hunting, recreational use, and for other lawful purposes.

The right of a parent to determine what medical procedures will be performed on their child: the right to determine the type of schooling their child will receive, Homeschooling being the preferred method; The right of a parent to discipline their child especially spanking; The right of a property owner, as long as he conforms to the States environmental laws, to determine what is to be done with said property especially in regard to vegetation grown and the esthetics of Dwellings and landscaping, restricting only vulgarity and immorality; Shall not be infringed.

The right of the people to be secure in their persons, houses, papers, and effects (any property or curtilage), against unreasonable searches and seizures, shall not be violated, and no Warrants shall issue, but upon probable cause, supported by Oath or affirmation, and particularly describing the place to be searched, and the persons or things to be seized. This is binding on all government agencies.

Neither slavery nor involuntary servitude, **Except** as a punishment for crime whereof the party shall have been duly convicted, shall exist within the United States, or any place subject to their jurisdiction.

All male citizens, except those Persons attainted and incarcerated for crimes committed, being twenty years of age shall not be denied the right to vote; No male citizen may be drafted who has not obtained the age of twenty, but may volunteer at the age of eighteen.

No Soldier shall, in time of peace be quartered in any house, without the consent of the Owner, nor in time of war, but in a manner to be prescribed by law.

The enumeration in the Constitution, of certain rights, privilege and immunities (and immunities shall mean **Exemption** from any **Charge**, **duty**, office, **tax, or imposition),** shall not be construed to **Deny** or **Disparage** others retained by the people.

The right to recall a Representative of their State by the people, or a Senator by the State shall not be abridged.

The right of male citizens of the United States to vote in any election for President or Vice President, for electors for President or Vice President, or Representative in Congress, shall not be denied or abridged by the United States or any State by reason of failure to pay poll tax or other tax.

The powers not delegated to the United States by the Constitution, nor prohibited by it to the States, are reserved to the States respectively, or **to the People**.

Article 2

Section 1

The executive Power shall be vested in a President of the United States of America. He shall hold his Office during one Term of six Years, and, together with the Vice President, chosen for the same Term, be elected, as follows.

Each State shall appoint, in such Manner as the Legislature thereof may direct, a Number of Electors, equal to the whole Number of the most numerous Branch of the State Legislature: but no Senator or Representative, or Person holding an Office of Trust or Profit under the United States, shall be appointed an Elector.

The Congress may determine the Time of choosing the Electors, and the Day on which they shall give their Votes; which Day shall be the same throughout the United States.

One month prior to the Electoral Vote, a Populace Vote, in which all male citizen twenty years of age, and eligible to vote, shall vote for one candidate listed for President and one candidate listed for Vice-President and the five candidates with the most votes for President and the five candidates with the most votes for Vice-President shall move on to the Electoral Vote. The Electors shall meet in their respective states and vote by ballot for President and Vice-President, one of whom, at least, shall not be an inhabitant of the same state with themselves; they shall name in their ballots the person voted for as President, and in distinct ballots the person voted for as Vice-President, and they shall make distinct lists of all persons voted for as President, and of all persons voted for as Vice-President, and of the number of votes for each, which lists they shall sign and certify, and transmit sealed to the seat of the government of the United States, directed to the President of the Senate; -- the President of the Senate shall, in the presence of the Senate and House of Representatives, open all the certificates and the votes shall then be counted; -- The person having the greatest number of votes for President, shall be the President; and if no person have such majority, and two or more have the same number of votes, then from the persons having the highest numbers not exceeding three on the list of those voted for as President, the House of Representatives shall choose immediately, by ballot, the President. But in choosing the President, the votes shall be taken by states, the representation from each state having one vote; a quorum for this purpose shall consist of a member from two-thirds of the states, and a majority of all the states shall be necessary to a choice. The person having the greatest number of votes as Vice-President, shall be the Vice-President, but if two or more have the same number of votes, the Senate shall choose the Vice-President; a quorum for the purpose shall consist of two-thirds of the whole number of Senators, and a majority of the whole number shall be necessary to a choice. But no person constitutionally ineligible to the office of President shall be eligible to that of Vice-President of the United States. All candidates for both President and Vice-President must have qualified prior to the vote of the electors.

No Person except a natural born Citizen, shall be eligible to the Office of President; neither shall any Person be eligible to that Office who shall not have attained to the Age of thirty-five Years, and been fourteen Years a Resident within the United States.

Section 2

If, at the time fixed for the beginning of the term of the President, being the second Thursday of January at Noon, the President elect shall have died, the Vice President elect shall become President.

Whenever there is a vacancy in the office of the Vice President, the President shall nominate a Vice President who shall take office upon confirmation by a majority vote of both Houses of Congress.

Whenever the President transmits to the President pro tempore of the Senate and the Speaker of the House of Representatives his written declaration that he is unable to discharge the powers and duties of his office, and until he transmits to them a written declaration to the contrary, such powers and duties shall be discharged by the Vice President as Acting President.

Whenever the Vice President and a majority of the principal officers of the executive departments, transmit to the President pro tempore of the Senate and the Speaker of the House of Representatives their written declaration that the President is unable to discharge the powers and duties of his office for reasons of mental instability or actions inconsistent of the well-being of this nation, Congress shall review the evidence and upon their concurrence, the Vice President shall immediately assume the powers and duties of the office as Acting President. The Vice-President shall have the power to convene both Houses when not in session for this purpose.

In Case of the Removal of the President from Office, or of his Death, Resignation, or Inability to discharge the Powers and Duties of the said Office, the Same shall devolve on the Vice President, and the Congress may by Law provide for the Case of Removal, Death, Resignation or Inability, both of the President and Vice President, declaring what Officer shall then act as President, and such Officer shall act accordingly, until a President shall be elected.

No person who has held the office of President, or acted as President, for more than two years of a term to which some other person was elected President, shall be elected to the office of President

Section 3

The President shall, at stated Times, receive for his Services, a salary, which shall neither be increased nor diminished during the Period for which he shall have been elected, and he shall not receive within that Period any other Emolument from the United States, or any of them.

Before he enter on the Execution of his Office, he shall take the following Oath or Affirmation:--"I do solemnly swear (or affirm) that I will faithfully execute the Office of President of the United States, and will to the best of my Ability, preserve, protect and defend the Constitution of the United States."

Section 4

The President shall be Commander in Chief of the Air Force, Army and Navy of the United States, and of the Militia of the several States, when called into the actual Service of the United States; he may require the Opinion, in writing, of the principal Officer in each of the executive Departments, upon any Subject relating to the Duties of their respective Offices, and give instruction, this being the extent of executive orders; and he shall have Power to grant Reprieves and Pardons for Offences against the United States, except in Cases of Impeachment and exile.

He shall have Power, by and with the Advice and Consent of the Senate, to make Treaties, provided two thirds of the Senators present concur; and he shall nominate, and by and with the Advice and Consent of the Senate, shall appoint Ambassadors, other public Ministers and Consuls, Judges of the supreme Court, and all other Officers of the United States, whose Appointments are not herein otherwise provided for, and which shall be established by Law: but the Congress may by Law Vest the Appointment of such inferior Officers, as they think proper, in the

President alone, in the Courts of Justice, or in the Heads of Departments.

The President shall have Power to fill up all Vacancies that may happen during the Recess of the Senate, by granting Commissions which shall expire at the End of their next Session.

Section 5

He shall from time to time give to the Congress Information of the State of the Union, and **Recommend** to their Consideration such Measures as he shall judge necessary and expedient; he may, on extraordinary Occasions, convene both Houses, or either of them, and in Case of Disagreement between them, with Respect to the Time of Adjournment, he may adjourn them to such Time as he shall think proper; he shall receive Ambassadors and other public Ministers; he shall take Care that the Laws be faithfully executed, and shall Commission all the Officers of the United States.

At no time shall he dictate to Congress as to what laws will be drafted, or actions they are to take.

Section 6

The President, Vice President and all civil Officers of the United States, shall be removed from Office on Impeachment for, and Conviction of, Treason, Bribery, or other high Crimes and Misdemeanors.

Article 3

Section 1

The judicial Power of the United States shall be vested in one Supreme Court, and in such inferior Courts as the Congress may from time to time ordain and establish.

The Supreme Court shall convene once a year for nine weeks starting the second week in January and adjourn at the end of the first week in March. All Supreme Court Justices shall be appointed for one term of six years. The total number of Supreme Court Judges sitting on the bench shall not exceed seven. [Sources for nominees for the position of United States Supreme Court Justice will be any officer of the armed forces who has reached the rank of O-4, or any enlisted member of the armed forces who has reached the rank of E-7, and any law enforcement officer, State or federal, who has served honorably for at least 12 years.]

The Judges, of inferior Courts, shall hold their Offices during good Behavior, and all Judges shall, at stated Times, receive for their Services a Compensation, which shall not be diminished during their Continuance in Office.

Section 2

The judicial Power shall extend to all Cases, in Law and Equity, arising under this Constitution, the Laws of the United States, and Treaties made, or which shall be made, under their Authority;--to all Cases affecting Ambassadors, other public Ministers and Consuls;--to all Cases of admiralty and maritime Jurisdiction;--to Controversies to which the United States shall be a Party;--to Controversies between two or more States;--between Citizens of different States;--between Citizens of the same State claiming Lands under Grants of different States.

The Judicial power of the United States shall not be construed to extend to any suit in law or equity, commenced or prosecuted against one of the United States by Citizens of another State, or by Citizens or Subjects of any Foreign State.

In all Cases affecting Ambassadors, other public Ministers and Consuls, and those in which a State shall be Party, the Supreme Court shall have original Jurisdiction. In all the other Cases before mentioned, the Supreme Court shall have appellate Jurisdiction, both as to Law and Fact, with such Exceptions, and under such Regulations as the Congress shall make.

The Trial of all Crimes, except in Cases of Impeachment, shall be by Jury; and such Trial shall be held in the State where the said Crimes shall have been committed; but when not committed within any State, the Trial shall be at such Place or Places as the Congress may by Law have directed.

No inferior court of the federal government shall have the power to declare any Act, Law, Tax, or Duty unconstitutional. In any Case that a judge of an inferior court should deem the matter at hand to be in opposition to the Constitution of the United States, they shall appeal the case before the Supreme Court. All courts within the United States of America shall be Courts of Justice and not courts of law.

Bad Behavior by which a Judge shall be removed and or imprisoned Shall consist of, but not limited to; Hearing a case outside their venue and Jurisdiction, dictating new laws, (case law) which is in violation of Article 1, Section 1 of this Constitution, attempting to extend their authority beyond the courtroom, attempting to enforce judgments not supported by laws derived by the proper legislative body, attempting to overturn any law voted on by the majority of the people or laws of the several States, and consistently making poor decisions or a decision that is an offence to this nation's heritage or is contradictive to this Constitution. The Historical reasons for impeachments shall be considered as well when determining what bad behavior is.

Case Law and Precedence are strictly forbidden anywhere within the United States of America and at any level of government. Each case must be judged on its own merits.

The President of the United States shall have the authority to remove any judge of an inferior court, in violation of the aforementioned reasons, from his office without the consent of Congress. The House of Representatives must consent by a majority vote in the case of removal of a Supreme Court justice for an impeachment. In Addition, the Executive of the State in which an offending judge presides, and/or the People of that State by a majority vote, may remove an inferior court Judge of the United States or judge of the several States, for the afore mentioned reasons.

Section 3

No person shall be held to answer for a capital, or otherwise infamous crime, unless on a presentment or indictment of a Grand Jury, except in cases arising in the land or naval forces, or in the Militia, when in actual service in time of War or public danger; nor shall any person be subject for the same offence to be twice put in jeopardy of life or limb; nor shall be compelled in any criminal case to be a witness against himself, nor be deprived of life, liberty, or property, without due process of law; nor shall private property be taken for public use, without just compensation.

In all criminal prosecutions, the accused shall enjoy the right to a speedy (not exceeding ninety days from indictment to final appeal) and public trial, by an impartial jury of the State and district wherein the crime shall have been committed, which district shall have been previously ascertained by law, and to be informed of the nature and cause of the accusation; to be confronted with the witnesses against him; to have compulsory process for obtaining witnesses in his favor, and to have the Assistance of Counsel for his defense.

In Suits at common law, where the value in controversy shall exceed twenty dollars, the right of trial by jury shall be preserved, and no fact tried by a jury, shall be otherwise re-examined in any Court of the United States, than according to the rules of the common law.

Excessive bail shall not be required, nor excessive fines imposed.

The historical reference of cruel and unusual punishments as stated in the Constitution of 1789 referred to devices and practices such at Racking, the Iron Maiden and Hang, Draw, and Quartering. Capital punishment is the just and proper punishment for; murder, manslaughter, rape, sodomy, kidnapping, infant and toddler molestation; and corporal punishment in conjunction with or in lieu of incarceration consisting of no more than forty strikes of a flogging strap, or twenty-five strikes of a bullwhip, and no more than fifteen strikes of a paddle for a juvenile.

Section 4

Treason against the United States, shall consist in levying War against them, or in adhering to their Enemies, giving them Aid and Comfort; or in elected officers, or persons bribing elected officers, acting in concert, or solely to undermine the principles of this constitution, rebelling with the intent to establish an inferior form of government, primarily the Marxist forms of government. No Person shall be convicted of Treason unless on the

Testimony of two Witnesses to the same overt Act, or on Confession in open Court.

The Punishment of Treason shall be death by hanging, but no Attainder of Treason shall work Corruption of Blood, or Forfeiture except during the Life of the Person attainted.

Article 4

Section 1

Full Faith and Credit, or more plainly, all Authority, shall be given in each State to the public Acts, (these are all Acts and laws dealing with the affairs of the people such as housing, labor, retirement, education, health, etc.) public Records, to include all taxation records, and judicial Proceedings of every other State. And the Congress may by general Laws prescribe the Manner in which such Acts, Records and Proceedings shall be **Proved**, and the **Effect** thereof. No such law shall exceed three paragraphs in length, the first describing the concern of congress, the second describing what Manner the states shall prove their laws exist, and third manner of proof for the effectiveness of said laws, and any penalty to the State not in compliance.

The only record and Identification the United States government shall be able to maintain is the United States Pass Port, and a national crime information database accessible to all Law Enforcement.

Section 2

The Citizens of each State shall be entitled to all Privileges and Immunities of Citizens in the several States.

A Person charged in any State with Treason, Felony, or other Crime, who shall flee from Justice, and be found in another State, shall on Demand of the executive Authority of the State from which he fled, be delivered up, to be removed to the State having Jurisdiction of the Crime.

Section 3

New States may be admitted by the Congress into this Union; but no new State shall be formed or erected within the Jurisdiction of any other State; nor any State be formed by the Junction of two or more States, or Parts of States, without the Consent of the Legislatures of the States concerned as well as of the Congress. All lands within the established Boarders of the State shall become the property of the State, and no Act by Congress may retain any portion of the land, and the United States may only obtain lands as prescribed in Article One, Section Eight of this Constitution, and for the reasons enumerated.

The Congress shall have Power to dispose of and make all needful Rules and Regulations respecting the Territory or other Property belonging to the United States; and nothing in this Constitution shall be so construed as to Prejudice any Claims of the United States, **or** of Any particular State.

Section 4

Each State within this Union is a Sovereignty of itself, and The United States shall guarantee to every State in this Union a Republican Form of Government, and shall protect each of them against Invasion; and only on Application of the Legislature, or of the Executive (when the Legislature cannot be convened), against domestic Violence. At no other time shall the United States interfere with the affairs of the Several States.

Section 5

No State shall enter into any Treaty, Alliance, or Confederation; grant Letters of Marque and Reprisal; coin Money; emit Bills of Credit; make anything but gold, silver, and copper Coin a Tender in Payment of Debts; pass any Bill of Attainder, ex post facto Law, or Law impairing the obligation of contracts that are **Negotiated** and agreed upon by two parties, or grant any Title of Nobility.

No State shall, without the Consent of the Congress, lay Imposts or Duties on Imports or Exports, except what may be absolutely necessary for executing it's inspection Laws: any revenue from the net Produce of all Duties and Imposts, laid by any State on Imports or Exports, exceeding the need of executing inspections, shall be for the Use of the Treasury of the United States.

No State shall, without the Consent of Congress, lay any Duty of Tonnage, keep Troops, or Ships of

War in time of Peace, enter into any Agreement, or Compact with a foreign Power, or engage in War, **Unless** actually invaded, or in such imminent Danger as will not admit of delay.

Article 5

The Congress, whenever two thirds of both Houses shall deem it necessary, shall **Propose** Amendments to this Constitution, or, on the Application of the Legislatures of two thirds of the several States, shall call a Convention for proposing Amendments, which, in either Case, shall be valid to all Intents and Purposes, as Part of this Constitution, when ratified by the Legislatures of three fourths of the several States, or by Conventions in three fourths thereof, as the one or the other Mode of Ratification may be proposed by the Congress with the consent of the States; and that no State, without its Consent, shall be deprived of its equal Suffrage in the Senate.

Article 6

Because of the corruption of the former bureaucrats running this nation, All Debts contracted and Engagements entered into, before the Adoption of this Constitution, shall be voided. All illegal entities although enacted by Congress but repugnant to the United States Constitution of 1789, claiming interest owed for loans on an illegal currency (fiduciary or fait) shall be tried for treason and put to death. All treaties shall be renegotiated.

This Constitution, as an extension of the Declaration of Independence, and the Laws of the United States which shall be made in Pursuance thereof; and all Treaties made, or which shall be made, under the Authority of the United States, that is, this Constitution, **shall be the Supreme Law of the Land**; and the Judges in every State shall be bound thereby, any Thing in the Constitution or Laws of any State to the Contrary notwithstanding, or in other words, are null and void. To Clarify; every State, County, Parish, Municipality, and even Home Owners Association is bound to this Constitution and the laws made under its authority. The Senators and Representatives before mentioned, and the Members of the several State Legislatures, and all executive and judicial Officers, both of the United States and of the several States, shall be bound by Oath or Affirmation, to support this Constitution; but no religious Test shall ever be required as a Qualification to any Office or public Trust under the United States.

In Accordance with Article VI of this Constitution, All aspects of the Constitution of the United States shall be strictly adhered to, and in addition to Impeachment as prescribed in Article Two, Section Six of this Constitution, any civil officer of the United States to include judicial Officers both of the Supreme and inferior courts, Senators and Representatives, the President and Vice President, and the Members of the several State Legislatures, and all executive and judicial officers of the several States who are found in violation of this Constitution shall be Indicted, tried, judged, and punished, subject to imprisonment of up to ten years and fined up to $50,000.00.

In all cases in which the Death penalty is required by this Constitution, the person shall be charged with treason, and the convicted shall hang by the neck at the gallows until dead, and no other form of execution shall be permitted, but for the President of the United States, as he is the Commander and Chief of the Armed Forces, he may choose the option of death by firing squad. The courts shall have Thirty days to complete this requirement.

Any and all Laws, Offices, or Agencies, past, present, or future, formed outside the confines and in violation of the Constitution of the United States, are null and void.

The Supreme Court, the Supreme Courts of the Several States, the President, the Executive of the several States, and a jury shall have the authority to declare an Act, Law, Tax, or Duty enacted by the Congress of United States, unconstitutional, and the people shall retain the right to petition these entities directly for redness of constitutional grievances.

Article 7

The Executive Branch shall consist of six Departments.

The Department of Defense, Which shall govern the branches of the Armed Forces, Veteran Affairs and support agencies;

The State Department, which shall govern Ambassadors, other public Ministers and Consuls, the Law of Nations, and Foreign Affairs;

The Treasury Department, which shall govern the minting of Coin, national debt and or surplus, and revenues of the United States;

The Department of Interior, which shall govern Patents and Copyrights, Post Offices and postal routes, energy, communication, and all territories of the United States;

The Department of Justice, which shall govern the court system, and US Attorney's Office; and;

The Department Of Homeland Security, which shall govern all Law Enforcement agencies within the United States.

The Department of Homeland Security shall be comprised of;

The US Marshall Service whose primary responsibility will be to investigate any crime or accusation of a crime committed by any judge of the United States as well as that of the Judges of the Several States and bring the offender to Justice. It shall also assist in prisoner extradition, fugitive recovery, Court Security, federal prison system, and witness protection.

The Immigration, Customs, and Border Protection Service whose responsibility will be the enforcement of all Immigration and Customs Laws, and;

The Federal Protective Service, whose responsibility will be to police all United States properties, and consist of the;

Investigation Division whose primary responsibility will be to investigate any crime or accusation of a crime committed by any Senator, or House Representative of the United States as well as that of the members of Legislature of the Several States and bring the offender to Justice, and to assist all State Law Enforcement agencies in cases crossing State lines, and multiple boundary jurisdictions, and the investigation of federal offences;

The Protection Service whose primary responsibility is the protection of the President, and other United State dignitaries, and shall investigate any crime or accusation of a crime committed by the President or Vice-President and bring him to justice, and;

The Police Division whose responsibility is for the security of all properties and territories of the United States, and to patrol all Postal Routes.

All evidence of Crimes committed by the President, Vice-President, Senators, Representatives, and Supreme Court Judges, and Judges of the inferior Courts, shall be brought before the House of Representative for Impeachment.

Article 8

The Ratification of the Conventions of thirty-eight States, shall be sufficient for the Establishment of

this Constitution between the States so ratifying
the Same.

As you can see the structure of the government is the same but
there are more ardent consequences for those who are willing to
violate this Constitution. In addition there are more enumerated
rights protected from the governments establishing greater freedoms
for the people and surer prosperity. Also the branches of government
no longer solely police themselves but now have additional overseers
to ensure compliance. What the founding father established was an
incredible document and should never be wholly abandoned if this
'Resolution' should occur. The modification that I made will help
insure that this nation will remain as our forefathers intended in
spite of future politicians.

NEW SYSTEM FOR VOTING

The prominent reason the plutocracy was able to commit such dastardly deeds was the political party line way of thinking we people have. Political parties are a very dangerous thing. The most dangerous thing about a political party is that once they are established, people tend to identify themselves with a party. Even when the parties' philosophical beliefs are drastically changed, people have erroneously committed themselves to a party even though that party no longer represents their beliefs. Soon, people will modify their beliefs to remain dedicated to the parties they have identified with even when those beliefs are contrary to their core values.

The Democratic Party is the prime example of this. It started out as the party that supported little to no government interference but became the party that demanded total governmental control. People such as Catholics who are revolted by the act of abortion are still dedicated members of the Democratic Party that adheres to the practice. This is insanity.

People, political parties developed so that like-minded politicians could band together for mutual support of their ideas. Also, it aided them in sharing financial burdens as well. As private citizens, we should never fall into the trap of identifying ourselves with any particular political party but rather be students of the various parties at election time to determine which party most closely represents our core beliefs and then vote accordingly. When that political party's values change, we are free to study the rival parties to determine which of them more closely aligns with our beliefs and elect representatives who reflect our values.

If we are not politicians, it is sheer foolishness for us to lay claim to be members of this or that party. If we have to label ourselves to achieve an identity, we can join a church, but we should never associate with a political party; they are too ambiguous a creature to depend on.

A sure way to reduce the possibility of a foreign agent infiltrating the governmental sphere is to do away with campaign contributions, which are nothing more than legalized bribery. Even if the contribution is going to the political party and not to a specific politician, the politician will still be obliged to concede favors to the contributor to appease the party. This we have seen in governmental bailouts after bailouts. It is out of our pockets that these illegal bailouts come from. And no, there is nowhere in the Constitution that permits the federal government to act as an insurance provider. These bailouts were criminal offenses performed by our members of Congress and presidents. That is what bribery always leads to.

I would like to prescribe a method of choosing a candidate for political office that does not require campaign contributions or our being bombarded by endless smear campaigns. Here is an example of a presidential election, but the method can be applied to all elections.

First, in an election year, from the first of May to the end of May, all interested parties who wish to run for president or vice president will submit their applications that have a brief narrative of what format the candidates are running under and what their concerns are and plans to address those concerns. If a candidate maligns another candidate in his narrative, that candidate is automatically pulled from the race.

Next, by mid-June, the government will send out a news pamphlet listing all the candidates with their narratives so all can start forming their opinions of the candidates. Right after that, the candidates will be required to fill out a questionnaire concerning their beliefs on the key issues of the day and what voting record they might have. Candidates who fail to complete the questionnaire are pulled from the race.

By mid-July, a second pamphlet containing the answers to the questionnaire is sent out, and the masses can read which candidates share their values.

By the first Tuesday in August, the government will sponsor televised debates of the presidential candidates for the people to see their potential choice in action. If any candidate attempts to malign another at this debate, that candidate will forfeit the race.

On the first Wednesday in August, there will be a vice presidential debate under the same rules. The same type of debates will be held again on the third Tuesday and Wednesday of August as well.

In September, each candidate will have a fifteen-minute televised interview to convince the people that he is the best choice. Again, candidates who malign a rival are expelled from the race.

At the end of September, the federal government will publish a background investigation on each candidate revealing pertinent information such as citizenship, residence, criminal activity, past election promises, and consequential voting record.

In the first week of October, a popular vote is conducted and the top five candidates with the most votes will move on to the electoral vote. Prior to the electoral vote, there will be one more debate and one more interview for each candidate to make his case. Then comes the electoral vote.

Also by law, the press will not be allowed to make commentaries on any candidate. The people should be free to make their decisions without propaganda.

With this method, each candidate will have an equal opportunity to persuade the people, and the people will have a greater opportunity to determine whom the best candidate for them is.

We need honest choices for candidates, not prearranged choices made for us by the powerful political system. If we wish to remain a free people, we better make our voices heard.

REFERENCES

The United States Constitution. (Read all of it. What it says is what it means.)

The Declaration of Independence. (Read all of it.)

The Federalist Papers 1–85.

Slater, Rosalie J. *American Dictionary of The English Language*, Noah Webster, 1828. San Francisco: The Foundation for American Christian Education, 2002. (Get a copy and if you ever need to look up a definition, use this as your reference.)

VIDEOS

Wall builders—The American Heritage Series by David Barton.

The John Birch Society—Overview of America and America Tyranny Step by Step, Saving our Republic. (Both outstanding organizations; check out all their resources.)

When Nations Die by Jim Nelson Black and Isaiah 3:12.

Halbrook, Stephen P. "Registration: The Nazi Paradigm." http://www.constitutionalisttnc.tripod.com/hitler-leftist/id14.html.

Holocaust, The\Shoah Page. "Hitler's Euthanasia Initiative." http://www.constitutionalisttnc.tripod.com/hitler-leftist/id16.html.

Hulsey, Martin G. "The Implication of Nazi Animal Protection." http://www.constitutionalisttnc.tripod.com/hitler-leftist/id11.html.

McNight, John J. "Gun Control Has Proven Record of Effectiveness." http://www.freerepublic.com/forum/a38d0fd5f403f.htm.

Precious-Life Ministries. "Hitler and Abortion." http://www.constitutionalisttnc.tripod.com/hitler-leftist/id15.html.

Ray, John J. "Hitler was a Socialist, & Modern Leftism as Recycled Fascism." http://www.constitutionalisttnc.tripod.com/hitler-leftist/id8.html.

Lively, Scott, with Kevin Abrams. "The Pink Swastika: Homosexuality in the Nazi Party." http://www.constitutionalisttnc.tripod.com/hitler-leftist/id12.html.

Lott, John R. Jr. "The Bias Against Guns." *American Hunter*. March 2004.

Britner, Richard. *Dark Side of America,* Redemption Press, 2006.

Hall, Verna M. *The Christian History of the Constitution of the United States of America*. San Francisco: Foundation for American Christian Education, 2001.

Hamburger, Kenneth E., Joseph R. Fischer, and Steven C. Gravlin. *Why America is Free*. Washington, DC: The Society of the Cincinnati, 1998.

Limbaugh, David. *Persecution*. Washington, DC: Regnary Publishing, 2003.

Davis, Peter. *The American Heritage Dictionary of the English Language*. New York: Dell, 1980.

Daniel, Clifton. *Chronicle of America*. New York: DK Publishing, 1997.

F. E. Compton Company. *Compton's Encyclopedia*. Division of Encyclopaedia Britannica, 1969.

Grussendorf, Kurt A., Michael R. Lawman, and Brian S. Ashbaugh. *United States History Heritage of Freedom, & America Land I Love.* Pensacola, FL: A Beka Book, 1994.

GSA Contract Guard Information Manual, Combating Terrorism, April 2001. Revision.

Home School Legal Defense Association. "Without Probable Cause." 20, no. 4 (July/August) 2004.

Newcomer, Alphonsa G., Alice E. Andrews, and Howard J. Hall. *Three Centuries of American Poetry and Prose.* Chicago: Scott, Foresman, 1917.

Strobel, Lee. *The Case for A Creator.* Grand Rapids, MI: Zondervan, 2004.

Printed in the United States
By Bookmasters